Life on the Off Ramp

Life on the Off Ramp

Most Family Life Occurs Far From the Fast Lane

Donna T Cavanagh

ISBN: 1-449-99700-7
EAN-13: 978-144999700-7

To my daughter, Coleen, and my wonderful dogs , Muffie, LuLu, and Frankie, who gave me so much material through the years.

Contents

Preface

This book is truly a life-long labor of love. I started writing my humor columns when my daughter was about five years of age. This spring, she graduates from Penn State University.

I have to say that during these years, my family were good sports as they were my main targets for material which wound up in local and national magazines.

Many of the essays I have left pretty much as they were written. Others I have edited a bit. Why? Because I am a writer, and no writer goes over her work without editing – no matter how many years have passed.

Life on the Off Ramp reflects the idea that most of us live our lives not in the fast lane, but on the off ramp where life is not quite as exciting. Our daily lives include many mundane events, but even in the most mundane events, humor abounds.

Fired Up for Summer

The Spring ritual remains the same. We open up the sun porch, uncover the resin furniture, put potting soil in the planters and, finally, we check the gas grill. But this year held a surprise. Our beloved grill was no more. It died over the winter, and immediately we felt the void in our lives. Each time my poor husband went out to the patio, he would emit a devastated sigh. I could see his heart was broken.

Finally, after two weekends of watching him grieve, I couldn't take it anymore. I announced, "Come on, let's go look at some gas grills."
Immediately, his face lit up. "Where should we go?" he asked in thunderous anticipation. "We should probably scout out as many stores as possible. We want to get the best grill at the best price."

You know, until this point, I didn't realize the bond which existed between this man and his gas grill. To me it's an appliance; to him it's a friend. And apparently, Edward isn't alone in this assessment. We went to one of the big home improvement stores, and we couldn't see the gas grills, because a wall of men -- about 40-men deep -- was surrounding them. We pushed ourselves forward to get a better view, and when we reached the front of the line, I heard my husband gasp. For there, standing in front of us, was the mother of all gas grills. I saw my husband's face, and then I looked around at the other men in the vicinity. Everyone of them wore the same look of amazement on his face as Edward did.

Yes, this grill had captured the attention of every male in that store. It had cast a spell and drew them all in. Frankly, as a woman, I was confused. I never drool over kitchen appliances this way. I view them as necessary evils. I have no desire to become attached to them. And I never see men drool over these appliances either. How come a man has trouble operating the stove in a kitchen, but put it outside and stick a propane tank under it, and he turns into the Galloping Gourmet?

So, here we were paying homage to this grill. I'll admit, it was impressive -- or at least massive. It was composed of three sections. The two end pieces were made of stainless steel and had burners and a mini-refrigerator attached to it while the center area had a stone foundation. This outdoor grill was more sophisticated than the real kitchen inside our house. Also attached to the grill were a cutting board, a rotisserie attachment and a spare propane tank. This baby also wore a price tag of $1,200.

When my husband lifted the lid of the grill, he drooled over the four levels of racks that sprung up and sparkled like chrome on a new car.

"Edward I love you from the bottom of my heart and soul, but there is no way in this lifetime you are spending that kind of money on a barbecue!" I said calmly.

"But, it would really come in handy when we have guests," he retorted.

"How many guests are you talking about? One? Two? The entire county?" I asked facetiously.

"You're right," he conceded. "We'll find something appropriate."

Now in agreement on what we wanted, we walked around looking at the other models. And there in the corner stood a nice, little, unpretentious grill. It stood there alone. No one crowded around it. My heart went out to it. It looked as if it needed a home and someone to care for it. None of the men in the store seemed to want it. It had no super duper grilling rack. It had no side burners or rotisserie. It wasn't even stainless steel. But what it did have was a price tag of 150 bucks. Now, I was in love.

"This one?" my husband asked incredulously. "But look at the difference. This has nothing -- not even a side burner to cook vegetables."

"Well, pardon me," I apologized. "Let's spend an extra $500 so you can stir beans at the same time you're cooking hot dogs. Be realistic. How would you put that other monstrosity together?"

It was then I saw the light bulb click on over his head. The assembly -- that was the key. He forgot about the assembly. Edward hates putting gas grills together.

"Okay, you're right," he admitted quickly. "A smaller grill will be better for us. But let's not buy it right now. Maybe we should look around more and see if there's a better deal."

I agreed for I know he's hoping that somewhere in some store is his dream grill, already assembled and selling for no more than $300. I'll let him dream on for a while. He deserves it because as we all know, the relationship between a man and his barbecue is sacred.

Even Barbie's Beauty Must Fade

When I read recently that Mattel was going to "redo" Barbie, I initially felt a twinge of sadness. Once again, I thought, our insatiable quest for reality was about to destroy another icon. But as I pondered the toy company's move further, I began to think that maybe it was time for Barbie to change. Maybe it was time for the 38-year-old bombshell to embrace middle age like the rest of us.

While I am sure that Barbie will weather getting older better than most other women on face of the planet, I think she still deserves our sympathy for she will face challenges that she never knew existed. For starters, Barbie is going to have to accept wider hips. Yep, Mattel has discovered that "real" women become broader in the hip area as they age. Who knew? Thank God, Mattel is around to tell us this. We women sure would have never figured that one out. Also, Mattel has decided that the "new "Barbie will exhibit a smaller bust line and a thicker waist -- once again -- traits of real, live women.

I do admit that deep inside my soul, I feel a sense of satisfaction knowing that Barbie is about to lose that perfect body that has fired up the imaginations of every male doll and real man on Earth for the past forty years. But I also have to admit that part of me flinches when I realize that I'm the thicker waisted, wider hipped, smaller busted real woman Mattel is talking about.

Ick! When did this all happen? And you know what? I never would have noticed all these body changes if Mattel didn't feel compelled to inform me about them. I was living happily in denial until this whole Barbie thing erupted.

So, I need to ask, "Who felt the need to ruin my self image?"

I have heard a lot of women saying that the old Barbie exploited the female gender. The old Barbie gave men an unrealistic idea of what women look like. And worse, the old Barbie gave little girls an unrealistic view of what adulthood will look like on them. Well, to an extent I agree with this. Little girls have to learn that beautiful women come in all shapes and sizes. They have to learn that beauty is determined by the size of a woman's heart -- not the size of her breasts or how much she weighs. But I don't think Mattel alone is going to teach girls this. I think this is a job for someone bigger than Barbie. Last I looked, Barbie didn't have that much power.

But, maybe Barbie is the starting point. Maybe we should make all dolls and toys resemble the average human being. Mattel should start a trend. Along with Barbie, the company should now transform Ken from the tall, perfect-haired model into a stocky, balding doll with thick eyebrows and a beer belly. Let's face it. If we're going to teach little girls that they can't look like Barbie forever, we might as well teach them that we can't date men like Ken forever either.

Okay, don't get upset. I didn't mean to attack Ken. Maybe I'm taking this Barbie thing too seriously. After all she is a doll right? I guess then the new Barbie won't care when she discovers that she doesn't fit into any of the clothes her predecessors wore. Once again, I have to confess, I have a sadistic urge to watch the first Barbie go shopping for a bigger size wardrobe.

I wonder if she'll stand in the mirror and scream, "Be gone, damned fat, be gone." M Maybe, if Barbie gets a little too overweight, Mattel can come up with some kind of diet food for her, and we can watch Barbie slim down before our eyes. She could be our weight control guru. It can't be that hard. She already has a fitness video out.

You know this plumper Barbie could also lead to new products which reflect the changing American woman. Next, Mattel can make a Barbie with cellulite and then a Barbie with wrinkles. And finally there can be a "Gray Away Barbie" - a doll which comes with her own hair dye to conceal gray hair.

These ideas sound pretty stupid huh? I think before we reform all the toys in the world to reflect real life, we need to remember who plays with these dolls. While I don't believe we should lie or misguide kids, I don't think we have to shock them into reality from day one. Let them dream. Wider hips, thicker waists and sagging bust lines are going to come no matter what, why ruin the mystery for them?

The Bathroom

A few months ago, my husband and I decided to convert our powder room into a full bath. I don't know why we decided to do this project. It was not on the to-do list anywhere. But one Sunday, as Edward was looking through the pile of home improvement store circulars, he mentioned that he would like to change the floor tile in that bathroom. I agreed that new floor tile was a good idea. Then I pondered further.

"You know what I would really like to do to that bathroom?" I asked dreamily. "I would like to change the entrance so you enter it through the family room instead of the laundry room."

"Why? What's the difference how you get into it?"

"The difference is anytime we have guests, I have to stuff the clothes from the laundry room into plastic bags and hide them in the closets so no one thinks we're slobs."

"Why do you care? We are slobs," he declared in a matter-of-fact voice.

"I am not a slob," I argued defensively. "I am just time challenged. Laundry doesn't fit into the schedule anymore."

Edward gave me a quizzical look, but I knew he was caving. I took advantage of his vulnerability.

"Don't you think that it's a bit strange to have the guest powder room off the laundry room anyway? It's pretty safe to say a man must of have designed this house. No woman in her right mind would consent to that idea.

It's just plain stupid. Who invites the whole world to see their dirty laundry?"

While he wasn't impressed with my logic, he knew I was about ready for a round of man bashing, and he was losing ground. Then, I finished him off with a more practical approach.

"You know, if you didn't have to go into the laundry room to get to that bathroom, you would forget those clothes were even there. You would never be reminded to fold a load of laundry or put some dirty ones in the washer. You probably wouldn't have to set foot in that laundry room unless it was an emergency."

I could see my husband liked this idea.

"Okay, let's do it, and while we're at it, let's see how much it costs to add a shower."

Immediately, Edward went to retrieve his tape measure. He took measurements. He made sketches. He explained his remodeling plan. He was an engineer in action. Then it was up to me to find a contractor.

I interviewed five contractors. One came in a suit and tie and stayed for three hours. He drank coffee and talked fixtures. I was bored. He promised me a written estimate in 10 days. I'm still waiting.

That night I had a contractor dream. I dreamed that a man with dark, curly hair came to the door to give me an estimate. Also in my dream, the man came back and robbed me blind in the middle of the night. I laughed at that dream until the following afternoon, when the next contractor came to my door. He had dark, curly hair and looked just like the guy in my dream. Needless to say, I didn't hire him. I felt badly about it. I am not a superstitious person, but that was too much of coincidence -- even for me.

Finally, we found Bruce. He was polite and personable, and my dog loved him. He worked with his brother, and they did a great job. They even fixed my other toilet for free when it overflowed while they were in the house. I wanted to adopt them by the time the project was over. Alas, they had to move on to other remodeling jobs. But I took solace in the fact that I had a whole new bathroom, and I didn't even know I wanted it. What's the most enjoyable feature of that bathroom? It's not the tile or the shower or the pretty stenciling. It's the fact that when I go into that bathroom, I don't see piles of clothes begging to be washed, dried or ironed. Yes, I can go into that bathroom free of guilt. Who would have thought that one bathroom -- one little bathroom --could give me so much pleasure?

The Bathing Suit Experience

The time has come, and there is no turning back. I must dig deep within myself and face the challenge bravely. I know it won't be easy, and I know it won't be pretty. But, I also know, I have put it off as long as possible. I must go buy a bathing suit.

Do I sound a tad melodramatic? If I ask this question to most women, the answer is no. Bathing suit shopping represents one of the most painful experiences women can endure. I'm not sure, but I think I read somewhere that women consider only childbirth more uncomfortable. Okay, that statement may be an exaggeration, but I know of no woman who looks forward to this activity. And can you blame us?

When we wear a bathing suit, we reveal to the world everything we've tried to hide all year. We can no longer conceal our little imperfections as we do when we wear a multi-layer, winter ensemble. The summer is the season for letting it all hang out, and like it or not, there's no way around it. But that doesn't mean we won't try.

In recent years, I have seen manufacturers advertise tummy-slimming and hip-hiding bathing suits. Initially, I considered these suits to be the greatest products ever invented -- until I purchased one. The first few hours, I was comfortable with my instantly slender self. By hour three, I realized my very breath was being squeezed out of me. The suit was like a spandex boa constrictor. I thought for sure I was a goner.

One of my friends who thinks she has a masculine build bought herself a bust-building, buttock-enhancing suit. I saw the padding in this garment, and I laughed. She ignored my callousness and wore the suit to the beach proudly. All was going well until her husband innocently commented that it looked as if she glued a beach ball on to her derriere. The next day, the suit was in the trash, and her husband was atoning for his remark at the jewelry store.

Do you see the dangers behind bathing suits? Loved ones and marriages are threatened by their very existence. Men must watch every word they utter when their wives and female friends put on these garments.

When a woman dons a bathing suit, a man dons a suit of armor. I have been married for many years. And only once in these many years, has my husband dared to evaluate my body in a swimsuit. It only took one offhand remark and one round of my tears for him to learn his lesson. In his mind, commenting on a bathing suit is a no win situation for any man. Today, he might think to himself that I look like one of the Baywatch babes in a swimsuit, but he would never tell me. Why? Because the scenario that would follow would shake the very foundations of our relationship. It would go something like this.

"Wow, you look great in that suit. You look like that Pamela Anderson."

"You're such a liar. You're just saying that because my thighs and hips look fat. They do, don't they?"

"No, I swear. I mean it. You look okay. "

"Just okay? See, you think I am fat. By the way, you're not allowed to watch that lifeguard show with those big-chested girls in those skimpy one piece suits anymore. It's off limits in this house. Hand over the remote."

Although a fictional situation, it is a possible one, and it does illustrate why men avoid the topic of women's bathing suits at all costs -- at least when they're talking to women. So, what's the answer? We women could just accept our bodies and realize that most of us are not going to look like the models in the swimsuit catalogs. Hell, those models don't even look like they do in the swimsuit catalogs. It's amazing what stage makeup and a good airbrush will do.

I think we have one more option besides acceptance: Deception. This is how it would work. All the stores in the world install special mirrors in their fitting rooms. These mirrors make every woman look as if she were a size eight or ten. I'd say a size four, but that's not deception for the great majority of us -- that's hallucination. But seeing a svelte image in the mirror would make us feel more secure with our appearance, and the men in our lives would sleep without fear of saying the wrong thing or being forced to partake of some weird crash diet. I understand that this plan of deception is somewhat irresponsible. Speaking for just me, I'm willing to live with this irresponsibility. What can I possibly lose -- except maybe 25 pounds from my imagination?

Back to School Blues?

I was getting my eyebrows waxed when the woman who was doing the waxing started to make conversation. Usually, I'm not a big talker when someone is ripping the hair off my eyelids, and I have my reasons for this: First, I want the person who is applying the hot wax to devote all her attention to this task. I don't want her to be distracted. That's just me. Secondly, I think it is risky expressing a difference of opinion to a person who has the potential to cause me a lot of pain -- on purpose.

Anyway, this woman started to talk about the upcoming school year and her expectations for her kids.

"Are you looking forward to sending your kids off for another year?" she asked politely.

"I don't know. Are you?" I asked back with appropriate caution hoping she'd tell me what my correct response should be.

"No. I miss the kids dearly when they're not at home."

"Okay, me too."

I admit it, I have no spine. This was a total lie. It was mid-August, and at this point in the summer, I couldn't wait for my daughter to go back to school. I was not only counting down the days, I had counted down the hours and the minutes. But I certainly wasn't going to confess this to the Mother of the Year who had my eyebrows at her mercy and a canister of molten wax in her possession.

I decided I would tell her the truth when the waxing danger had passed, but I soon changed my mind. Apparently, this woman really does miss her kids all day long. I thought it was not my place to question her devotion. In fact, I began to worry about my lack of it.

Don't get me wrong. I love my daughter completely. I, like most mothers, would give up my life for her. But by mid-summer, I've had enough. I've had enough of the activities, the pool, the never-ending desire to play, the sleepovers and the extended bedtime. I'm exhausted from the worry I expend each time she goes out of the house to swim, skate or ride her bike. When she's in school, I don't have this constant fear that she's biking too far from home or taking too many daring jumps off the high dive. When she's in school, I get my work done, and there is never that cry that comes so often in the summer,

"Mom, I'm bored. There is nothing to do."

Okay, so a lot of moms don't want to say they like shipping their kids off to school for six hours a day. But that is what the majority of moms feel. How can you tell? Look around when moms are with their kids shopping for school supplies and clothes. The kids are miserable; the moms are smiling. Never does a mother demonstrate so much patience with a child as when she is shopping for school stuff. Another clue: mothers take on an eerie, calm demeanor around the end of August. The nervous edge is gone from their voices. Their faces appear serene. It's as if they have made it through the darkness, and now the light at the end of the tunnel is there for them to behold.

And what about these moms who cry every year on the first day of school? What do the rest of us do when they moan and groan about the cruelty of being separated from their children every day? We could comfort them and tell them everything is going to be fine; or, we could knock some much needed sense into them. These women ruin the first day of school celebrations for the rest of us. They bring sadness and despair where there should be joy and exultation. There should be a rule which bans parental tears on any school property.

Tears don't help anyway. Sure, I cried the first day my daughter got on the bus to go to Kindergarten. I even followed that bus to make sure she got to school safely. Yes, it was tough. But I like millions of mothers got through it. And what did we learn from this experience? We learned that it's no good to hold on to our kids too long because if we do, they'll never be strong or confident or independent. And worst of all, they'll never want to leave home. And life will turn into one very long summer.

The Bad Cat

Recently, my friend, Ginny, called to postpone a lunch date. The reason for the delay: she had to take her cat to the cardiologist. I'm sorry, but when she first told me this, I burst out laughing. I know how insensitive that sounds especially since I'm an animal lover. But I never even knew there were cat cardiologists.

Apparently her cat had a major heart problem and she had to take her for an EKG and further testing. I have to admit I was intrigued.

"Do they do the same tests as humans? Do you think she'll have to run on a tread mill with wires attached to her?" I asked somewhat maliciously. "How do they make her run? Do they put a fake bird at the end and tell her to chase it?"

Apparently, Ginny hadn't thought about this, and the image of her old cat on the treadmill even made her giggle.

"Don't make me laugh," she scolded me. "This is serious. After all, I've had Casey since before I was married. She's special to me."

Now, before everyone out there gets all misty over this cat, let me describe this feline from hell. First of all, she only likes women. Correction: she only likes two women -- Ginny and her daughter, Jessica. She barely acknowledges Ginny's husband, Mike and their son, Tim. According to the cat, the only purpose the men folk have is that of a trampoline. It seems Casey likes to pounce upon them in the middle of the night when their guard is down and they're sleeping peacefully. She pounces, they awaken, and she hisses in their faces sending them screaming into the night.

Casey also has no tolerance for the family dog, Jake. Jake is constantly at this animal's mercy. And you the funny thing about this? Jake is a big, big dog. He howls, he jumps, he barks, but when the cat comes near him, he quakes with fear just like the rest of the world.

This cat's congenial personality has also made a reputation for itself outside the family home. For example, Ginny greets people at the door with "Come on in, but don't go near the cat, she's mean, and she bites."

So, is it any wonder why guests cower on the living room furniture when the cat goes into a stalking position, circling around them, producing sounds that mimic those of that girl in the movie "The Exorcist". Most of us who have witnessed this cat in action swear that somewhere in that 12-pound body is a 500-pound Bengal tiger ready to attack.

The family vet has also had his problems treating the cat. The word "belligerent" is listed all over Casey's chart. A few years back, the vet prescribed tranquilizers for her so that she could adjust to living next to other breathing beings --especially Jake. Everyday, Ginny had to give this animal a half of a valium. I've told Ginny often that if I were her and I had this animal, I would take the other half. Why should that cat be the only one in a good mood?

But, Ginny still insists that the cat is special. For sixteen years, that cat has been an important part of her life. Casey has been queen of the roost, and she has known it. But now, as Casey enters the twilight days of her life, I say to Mike,

"Well, how long can the cat live?"

And Mike responds with a sense of resignation. "This cat? Forever! I'll be dead before her. And that's just what she wants."

So, when it comes time for the decision about what to do about Casey, Ginny will have to make that decision on her own because she knows very few people in this world will opt for extending this cat's life. As it is when Ginny talks to her friends about the possibility of ending Casey's existence, we say to her face, "Oh, that's too bad." But behind her back we're saying, "Thank God."

In Casey, Ginny had a true friend. Ginny could see past the biting, hissing, scratching and attacking when so many of us could not. Why? Because Ginny was never the recipient of any of this stuff. And so, in ending I say to Ginny, "I will cry with you when your beloved cat dies, but I will also go with you when you get another one -- just to make sure you don't find another cat just like Casey.

Christmas Cookies are Tough to Chew On

Each year I go through the same routine. About a month before Christmas, I take out my cookbooks and my cookie cutters and prepare to embark on a holiday bake off. I dream about creating gingerbread men dotted with raisins and icing. I imagine sugar cookies in the shape of snowmen, reindeer and Christmas trees. But despite my wishes and dreams, mainly what I create are big blobs of dough.

I can't explain how this happens. I follow the directions. I knead my dough thoroughly, I refrigerate that well-kneaded dough. I flour my cookie cutters. I do everything the cook books tell me to do. You would think that after years of practice, my cookies would look like real cookies. Instead, my gingerbread men look like they've gone three rounds with Mike Tyson, and my Christmas trees look as if they've been in one too many brush fires.

But each year I try. My husband and my daughter have learned to stay out of my way when I'm trying to bake. My friends have bake days with their children during the holidays. My family leaves town, and the dogs beg to go with them. When my daughter was little, before she went off to college, she was the one who warned my husband about the approaching bake off. Then the two of them would alert the fire department and take off for a two-day shopping spree.

"Daddy, we need to leave the house," she would say with a frightening tone in her voice. "There's real butter in the refrigerator -- lots of it. Do you know what that means? She's going to make cookies! We have to leave now, Dad! Now!"

From experience, my hubby has learned to heed this warning quickly. He used to ask if I was going to bake. He'd hint around that maybe that wasn't the best idea, and then he'd wait for my response which usually involved a few curse words and a remark about his lack of sensitivity towards me. This is how we knew our holiday season was in full swing.

While we savored this special Christmas tradition for many years, I think it may be time for a change. I think my family needs to break out of the old cookie mold -- so to speak -- and take on a new tradition: Boxed cookies.

I know buying cookies goes against every old-fashioned, Christmas tradition that exists. I know when I mention boxed cookies that baking women everywhere shake their heads at me and say, "Tsk, Tsk. There is nothing like the smell of Christmas cookies baking. "
You know what? I don't care. I'll burn one of those scented candles that smells like homemade cookies baking. I'm tired of bringing my homemade cookies to the houses of relatives and friends and watching as everybody laughs at them. I'm tired of putting hours into the baking process only to throw out my scorched creations into the trash. I'm tired of buying the rolled cookie dough with the designs already painted into the center and telling people that I made them from scratch.

Our Civil War

About two times a year, when my daughter visits my parents, my husband, Edward, and I take off for a weekend together. While some of you may be saying, "How romantic," allow me to explain. We don't go see the autumn foliage in Vermont, nor do we check into a quiet bed and breakfast in Cape May. No, we visit Civil War battlefields.

I know there are a great many of you civil war buffs out there, and I'm not mocking you. I, myself, love history; I love learning about history. But I have to tell you, I'm becoming far too comfortable sitting in the middle of cemeteries.

I have to admit, I have no else to blame for these weekends but me. I figured that visiting these battlefields was a good way to see the country and shop at antique stores; so, I encouraged this hobby. In fact, for our anniversary one year, I took him on the private tour of Gettysburg. You know, the one where you pay a guide to drive your car and for two hours he points out every blasted monument that exists in those 5,899.86 acres of park land. We have pictures of almost every one of those monuments from that tour and our many other visits to Gettysburg. We have more pictures of Gettysburg than we have of our wedding. My husband still writes to the guide. He talks about retiring out there, so he can be a tour guide. So, I ask him,

"Didn't they have good wars in Europe? Don't you want to see their battlefields too?"

He ignores me. You would think I would have learned a lesson from this. But, I'm not that smart. For his birthday that same year, I took him to see the four-hour movie, Gettysburg, which re-told the two-hour tour. In truth, it was a good movie. I was the only woman in the theater, and I didn't have to wait in line for the bathroom -- that was a definite plus. The only bad thing was I sat next to this civil war expert who insisted on whispering every military inaccuracy that could possibly exist in the flick. Finally, after an hour of being polite, I said to him,

"Look, I'm here to see Tom Berenger on the screen, okay? Please, stop talking to me."

My husband gave me a reproachful look as if I had broken some Civil War buff code. After intermission, he sat next to the man, and they had a great time.

The next trip he has planned is to Antietam, you know the sight of the bloodiest day in American history. This should be an uplifting experience. I'll have to remember my camera and some Prozac. And you know what's funny. I think we meet the same people at these sights. I think we all travel around together. I find that scary.

And what frightens me more are the chilling stories these people tell of seeing the ghosts of soldiers hiding in the woods or crouching in some field. So, I have implemented one rule when we do our Civil War visiting: I don't want to see any ghosts, spirits, or non-human entities. I don't care how friendly they are, I don't want to meet them. If I see just one, he goes on these trips alone.

I know many of you are asking, "It's a hobby, how much can it truly affect your daily life?"

Well, plenty. For example, my office is filled, and I mean filled, with Civil War books, and artwork. Edward owns every book which lists the 93rd New York regiment, his great-great grandfather's outfit. He wanted to display all this stuff in the living room or family room, but I selfishly objected, arguing it would clash with my decor. So, as a compromise the Civil War guys hang out with me while I write. It's a tad unnerving having all these military bigwigs from a century ago staring at you all day. I've learned to adjust to my office roommates. Maybe I should invite them to my next office Christmas party. I wonder if they'd show.

Needless to say, The Civil War is more than a hobby in our house. It's not that bad; at least it's an educational hobby. My daughter will benefit from it. When she gets a little older, and more able to comprehend the enormity of the Civil War, I'll make her come with us on our excursions to the battlefields. I'll consider it payback for childbirth.

The Days of Softball

Each spring, my husband, Edward coaches our daughter's softball team. I usually serve as an assistant coach. I do this because I like being involved. I also do this because I enjoy seeing that bewildered look my husband, the logical engineer, gets on his face when he interacts with his team of seven and eight-year old girls.

I would like to state now for the record that while Edward is a male, I don't consider him a sexist male. When he first started coaching, I don't think he thought coaching a group of girls would be any different than coaching a group of boys -- and for the most part, this proved true. Girls can accomplish as much as boys. They just do it with a bit more drama. With this said, I would like to outline for parents or any future coaches some of the observations Edward, myself and our loyal following of parents have made about little girls and the sport of softball.

1. Little girls don't like weather.

Wind, cold, rain, sun, heat-- everything bothers them. The sun gets in their eyes; the wind messes their hair; the cold makes them shiver; and a beautiful spring day makes them want to be somewhere else.

2. Players will not take the field if there are any insects within a one-mile radius.

Bees are especially troublesome. Players see bees buzzing in the grass, and immediately they panic. They do this frantic, dance ritual where they wave their arms and run around in circles all in an effort to avoid being stung.

What these girls don't know is that this hysteria is unnecessary. The bees aren't chasing the girls. They're lying in the grass, their nervous systems completely paralyzed from the high-pitched screams these girls emitted when they first saw the poor insects.

3. Little girls do not like the fashion behind softball.

The official softball pants are either too long or too short. The tee shirts are the wrong color or the wrong size for their bodies. They don't like wearing hats because they interfere with earrings and hairdos. The only reason why they tolerate the batting helmet is because they know they can't bat unless they wear that helmet. So, they will try on four or five helmets. They will physically fight each other for a certain helmet. They will wrestle each other to the ground to get a certain helmet.

4. Everyone wants to bat, but no one wants to field.

At the beginning of each inning, girls jump up and down screaming, "Is it my turn to bat yet?" But when it comes to go into the field, the request is more like, "Can I be on the bench this inning? Please, can I play the bench?"

All the motivational talks in the world about teamwork and learning to field that ball are lost on an eight-year-old who thinks it's too boring to stand in the field without anyone to talk to. Those who are forced to play, find ways to pass the time. Some eat their gloves, some pick dandelions and others do cartwheels.

Another interesting note about fielding: all commitment to the game ends when the players hear the ring of the ice cream truck. Twice this year, we've had to chase down players who left their positions screaming,

"It's the ice cream man! It's the ice cream man!"

In all fairness, even the batting team left to go chase down the truck. So, there we were: parents and coaches yelling after the children,

"Come back, now!! You can have ice cream later."

5. Many little girls do not like to chase balls that go pass them.

Most girls try to field the ball if it is in front of them, and many attempt to get pop-ups as well. But if the ball passes them and heads into the outfield, they will kiss that ball goodbye. Oh, sure, they'll turn and watch it travel into the distance. Some even wave to it. My husband runs into the outfield urging his players to come with him and get the ball. He looks like one of those people at the airport who signal the planes in. But do the girls come? No, they just stand there and look at him with this puzzled and insulted expression as if he told them to jump off a bridge. This is usually where I hang my head in frustration, and the crowd roars with laughter.

6. Little girls need to go the porto-potty about 18 times during a four-inning game.

And yes, they need to go in groups to a portable bathroom that is 15 feet away from the field. Truth be told, I like them going in partners in case one of them gets stuck, the other one can go for help. This has been known to happen.

7. Little girls are entertainers.

They make up cheers with well-choreographed steps. They sing songs while they wait to bat. They braid each other's hair. They serve juice and cookies to people in the stands. They bow, twirl and hug each other when they make a great play. You got to love these kids. When it comes down to it, spring would be pretty dull without them.

The Call of the Rescues

Recently, we had to put our German Shepherd, Miss Muffie, to sleep. She was my baby and my gentle giant. She guarded and loved us for 14 years, but alas, her time had come, and it was time to let her go. Her constant companion in our home was LuLu, another rescue pup who supposedly had a lot of German Shepherd in her gene pool. That was one shallow gene pool because there is not one sign of any shepherd in LuLu. She tips the scales at 38 pounds. I would like to say the rescue lied to us, but my brother took home LuLu's brother and he is about 50 pounds heavier and shepherdy looking. They do have the same mannerisms though, so we are just assuming LuLu was the runt of the litter. That is the only guess we have.

On a bravery scale of 1 to 10, LuLu lies about a negative 50. She is so afraid of everything from the sound of a plastic bag to the text ring on my cell phone. She also hates to be alone. When Miss Muffie passed away, I was not sure who was more upset, us or LuLu.

After a few weeks of LuLu looking lost, we thought we should check out the possibility of getting her a bodyguard dog. We headed back to a shelter that also had German Shepherd mix pups.

There we found Francesca Muffie (named after my mother and our Miss Muffie) or Frankie. Frankie was black and brown like Muffie and had huge paws. So, we knew she would be a big girl. She seemed timid and laid back, so I fell for her from the start. I sent a photo of her to my daughter who was away at Penn State, and she texted back, "Get her!"

After we got Frankie home, she got sick. At first I thought it was a simple puppy ailment, but it turned out to be Parvo which is often fatal. My local vet wanted us to put her down immediately, but we opted to help her fight. My daughter had finished finals, so she came home, and the three of us decided this dog was going to live and be with us. We couldn't lose two dogs in such a short time period. We moved her from the local vet to a great vet hospital in Plymouth Meeting, PA where they gave her transfusions and IVs of antibiotics. By day four, she was on the rebound, and as the vet said, had developed attitude. She returned to us in time for LuLu's birthday. LuLu still regards Frankie as the most annoying gift she has ever received.

A whole new Frankie came home after the Parvo. She was mischievous, demanding and growing by leaps and bounds. She is now an 80-pound lab/shepherd who thinks she is a lap dog. She has definitely become the dominant dog over LuLu who does not mind a bit-usually. Frankie can bully my LuLu too much sometimes, and this can cause what we call "Cujo" moments. These usually last a few seconds and ends with the two kissing each other's ears.

Frankie still needs more training. She is an explorer which means she is a flight risk. She has worked her way out of my fenced yard as well as my Mom's. LuLu has no desire to flee. She will dig a hole for Frankie to escape, but unless she is on a leash walking with us, she does not feel the need to have a meet and greet with the neighbors.

These dogs, like Miss Muffie, are spoiled. I have worked from home for years, so they have no clue what it's like not to have a stay-at- home Mom. I call them my employees. Usually, they get great annual reviews except that they tend to bark when I am trying to do interviews on the phone for articles I am writing. But they are great workers. They keep me company at lunch, and Frankie will even retrieve papers from the printer. LuLu hides when the printer goes on. Technology is not her thing.

It is funny how animals become such an important part of our lives. To this day, I tear up whenever I think of my Miss Muffie. I keep her ashes in the family room. We often say that Muffie sent Frankie to us, and that we were meant to save her. Each dog has had their own distinct personality, and each one we will always love. We never got the Beagle dog we thought we would get so many years ago. But I guess we got who we were supposed to get, and we have no complaints.

I'm Never Too Old to Rock and Roll?

On our last ladies' night out, I went with my friends to see John Cougar Mellencamp or John Cougar or John Mellencamp – take your pick in Camden, NJ. We were all excited about this outing.

As I was leaving the house, my daughter said, "Mom, I can't believe you're going to a concert. Aren't you too old?"

"No, contrary to what you may think, 36 is still considered young. Believe it or not, I still have my real teeth," I said sarcastically.

"Well, don't sing and dance so loud. Don't embarrass me."

"How many people do you know in Camden? I promise I won't embarrass you. If I see anyone I think you've had any contact with in life, I'll duck."

With that I left. As excited as I was over this event, I was a bit anxious. My daughter had struck a nerve. I hadn't been to a concert in 10 years. Maybe I was too old. I confessed my anxiety to my friends as we drove to the stadium. My friends admitted that they thought about the same thing, but we decided that was stupid. For although we were all in our thirties, we still felt 16 -- mentally anyway. So, it was okay to go and have a blast of a time.

I knew we were going to be fine from the moment we drove into the parking lot. It used to be when we went to concerts, the parking lots were filled with little sporty cars, convertibles, pickup trucks and motorcycles. This parking lot was a sea of minivans, station wagons and four-wheel drive vehicles. We couldn't locate anyone under 30. Sure, people were having tailgate parties, but there was no rowdy behavior. People weren't wearing ripped jeans and tank tops with no bras underneath them. No, people were in golf shirts, Dockers, and plaid shorts. Somehow, I got the feeling John Mellencamp was going to be disappointed in this crowd.

Where were his earthy fans with the tattoos and the straggly hair? These fans were eating fruit salad and talking on their cell phones.

We made our way to the lawn carrying a big blanket. As a teenager, I always liked lawn seats. On the grass, people would socialize and dance with each other all night long. It was always a great big party. We took the blanket and climbed up the concrete ramp that led to the lawn ready for the party that we were sure awaited us.

"God, this is steep," Mary said to me as she held on to my arm.

"Well, look at all the exercise our thighs will get," I whispered in an out-of-breath voice. "Did anyone notice where the bathrooms were?

"All the way at the bottom of the ramp," Linda huffed.

"Oh, God" Maryann said. "Maybe we'll only make one trip for beer."

Ten years ago, we would have danced and cart wheeled up that hill. Today, we held onto each other and joked how nice it would be if the stadium gave out oxygen at the top.

When we got to the lawn, we spread out blankets and then went to rent lawn chairs -- you know the ones with the high back for good support. We went back down the ramp for food and drink and were thrilled that we had to show our licenses in order to buy beer. We felt young and attractive until the beer stand worker told us they make even old people show their ID.

Before the concert started, we chatted and watched the people pass us by. We gaped at people who were a few years older than us who still dressed in hippie attire. We stared in amazement at some young woman who was almost not wearing a very skimpy outfit and wondered aloud if her parents knew she had left the house looking like that. Then the concert started, John Mellencamp came on the stage and the entire audience stood up and danced for hours. I didn't care if anyone I knew saw me. I didn't care if I embarrassed myself or my family. None of us did. We had fun watching the rock idol we used to drool over 10 years ago.

"He's still gorgeous, even if he's older," Maryann said.

"Yep, he's still a fetching fellow," I echoed . "I am so glad we did this."

"You know what? I heard Bryan Adams may be coming to play here soon," Maryann noted. "Anyone want to go?"

In one voice, the three of us shouted, "Count me in."

The Curse of Curls

Every six months or so I go to my hairdresser, Bernadette, and say, "Straighten out my hair."

And Bernadette who is always prepared for me says, "You don't want to straighten out your hair. People pay me a lot of money to get your hair."

To which I respond, "I'll give it to them for free. I want straight hair."

"Forget it," Bernadette shoots back. "It's not going to happen. You're stuck with it. Enjoy it and be grateful for it."

Those words have echoed in my ears since I was a little girl. And to anyone who has uttered these words to me, I can only say that I'm sorry. But I am not grateful for curly hair. To be grateful for curly hair means that I am thankful people often mistake me for Bozo the Clown's blonde twin. To be grateful for my hair means that I am thankful that on most days I look as if I stuck my finger into an electrical socket. To be grateful for my hair means that I have enjoyed the sarcastic comments of my family, friends, college roommates, husband and anyone else who through the years have had the pleasure of seeing me in the morning before I've had a chance to wet down my unruly mop.

It is for this lifetime of hair hell that I say emphatically, "I want straight hair!" I want hair that I can put up in a pony tail or an elegant bun. I want hair that doesn't need an hour-long blow drying session. I want to be able to air dry my hair without my head looking as if it's wearing a box of frizzy Brillo pads.

I know that many of you are saying that I am a shallow person for worrying about something so minor as hair. And the mature person in me agrees with this. But it's the childish side which reigns when it comes to matters of the hair. But I'm not the only one who feels this way. The hair care industry is booming. Countless numbers of men and women spend billions of dollars a year on shampoos, styling gels and conditioners. We all want our hair to look great. It's one of the first things people notice, and it's one of the first things they criticize.

Even my dear husband and daughter poke fun at my hair. They refer to my head as "The Bird's Nest". When things get lost in the house my daughter will shout with delight, "Look in Mommy's hair. Maybe it flew in there and got lost."

Being the good sport I am, I laugh at the jokes, and I nod in agreement when I hear my husband say, "It's just hair. What's the big deal? Look at me. Am I worried about my hair?"

And to his credit, he does not worry even though erosion has hit the top of his scalp. Rumor has it that his hair line isn't in the exact same place it was 15 years ago. But being the practical guy he is, Edward just throws up his arms and says, "That's how I'm made. That's how I'm staying."

I would love to be able to accept my hair this way. For the most part I try, but then a new product comes along, and I have to give it a shot. Two years ago, I tried this revolutionary hair treatment that promised to kill all curls. I spent $70 and two hours of my time sitting in a salon chair with chemicals that smelled a lot like bathroom cleaner oozing into my scalp. Yes, the stuff killed the curl -- for two days. After the two days, the curl came back curlier than ever. It was as if my head lashed out in vengeance at me for putting it through that torment.

After that experiment, I begrudgingly accepted my fate. Now, I sit back and watch with envy women who possess long, flowing hair. I still get angry that I can't wear a baseball cap or visor without the hair on the sides of my head bushing out four feet from my scalp. But most of all I get jealous when women with curly hair stand before me and say,

"I'm going to get my perm cut out today. I've had it with these curls. I feel like going straight for a while."

"Wow," I think to myself. "Life would be grand if I had that option."

Written Directions

It was the perfect plan. I was going to clean out my husband's closet before he got home from work. I estimated I had just about an hour to complete my assignment. I moved quickly. All was going well. Piles of his old clothes lay folded on the bed ready to be put into the cardboard storage box I bought at the store that morning.

"What a great idea," I told myself proudly as I ripped open the packaging that held my easy-to-assemble container. "He'll never even know I was in his closet."

As it turned out, he did know that I was in the closet. For when he came home, he found me sitting in the middle of a pile of clothes ripping apart a blue piece of mutilated cardboard which should have been my storage box.

"Are you having a bad day?" he asked sarcastically.

I flashed him my trademark drop dead glare and snapped,

"I can't get this stupid box together! I can't get slot A to fit into slot B!"

"That's because slot A doesn't go into slot B. If you read the directions, you would know that."

Again I gave him that drop dead glare. How dare he come home and accuse me of not reading the directions. Okay, if I think back on it, I didn't read the directions. But how was I supposed to know that a simple little piece of cardboard would cause so much trouble. What made the whole matter worse was that he put together the dumb box in less than two minutes -- all because he looked at the instructional diagram that came in the package. I tried to cover up my mistake by claiming that I like the challenge that comes along with not reading written directions, but that didn't seem to fly.

I admit it is pure impatience which keeps me from reading directions. I don't want to forage through some 80-page instruction book to find the answer to a simple problem. I want to ask a question and get the answer immediately. That's why I like the 800 help lines that come along with most new products today. I am a great believer in the "Why read directions when there's a live person on the other end of the phone just waiting to help me" philosophy.

This, of course, drives my husband crazy. He loves to read directions. He reads his driver's manual from cover to cover when he gets a new car. He knows where the windshield wiper fluid is before he leaves the car dealer. Me, I just wait until my window is covered over with gook and then I start flipping switches. While it is not the most practical method of operating a vehicle, it is the most exciting.

I think one of the reasons I'm so lazy about directions is that I know my husband has read everything I need to know about any appliance or gadget we have in the house. So, if I have a question, I call him up at work and ask him. He's usually pressed for time so he only gives me the information I absolutely need to know, and he doesn't put me on hold like those people on the 800 help lines.

However, his penchant for learning through written instruction has not always proved beneficial. My husband will never ask a store clerk where an item is located. He prefers to look at a directory. If a store doesn't have one, we wander the aisles aimlessly until he finds what he is looking for. This approach, he says, forces him to learn the store. Since I view this as a colossal waste of my time, I have taken steps to minimize these occurrences. Now, when I know he wants to look for a specific item at a store which does not post a directory, I call ahead. I not only ask if the store carries the product, but I ask where they keep it. Of course, I don't tell my husband I do this. I just let him think his superior sense of direction has triumphed again and has led him down the correct path.

The Dog

My husband and I both had dogs when we were children. So, it was only natural that we wanted our daughter, Coleen, to experience the same joy that we experienced with our pets. When she turned six, my sister Phyllis asked if she could do the honors and find the perfect pooch for our daughter. We readily agreed knowing that Phyllis would investigate thoroughly for not only was she an ardent dog lover but a professional researcher as well. We thought with those credentials, we couldn't miss finding a suitable canine.

For her convenience, we gave Phyllis a rough outline of our dream dog. We wanted a mutt that did little or no shedding and only a minimal amount of barking. Within weeks, Phyllis called with the good news.

"I have a beagle mix which should not grow to be more than 35 pounds. She's so cute, and she's short-haired so she won't shed," my sister cooed on the phone. "Coleen is just going to love carrying her all around."

I beamed with happiness. Coleen had already picked out a name for her dog months before, and now it seemed Miss Muffie was going to finally become a reality.

On Christmas morning, this six-pound little puppy with floppy ears came hopping out of a basket. She was such a teeny little bundle. We just adored her from the start even though I thought she looked different from other beagle puppies I had seen.

Our enthusiasm proved to be short-lived. That week we took her to the vet for her checkup. His first words out of his mouth stunned us.

"This is a nice-looking German Shepherd," he said to us nonchalantly while he examined the pooch. "You're going to be a big doggie."

"What do you mean?" I asked with an obvious alarmed shrill in my voice. "She's a beagle. They told my sister she was a beagle. They said she was going to be 35 pounds! Look at her -- she has all the coloring of a beagle!"

"Oh No!" he chuckled. "This is a shepherd. There's no beagle in this dog -- no beagle; only shepherd. She's going to be at least 85 pounds."

After I managed to breathe again, I ran home and promptly called my sister to relay this information.

"He must be wrong!" she said in disbelief. "Why would that woman who sold her to us lie?"

"I don't know, and I don't care," I answered calmly. "But the man went to veterinary school for years! "I think HE knows the difference between a beagle and a German Shepherd unlike some people!"

Well, there was a period of shock, but then we eventually resigned ourselves to the situation. We loved Miss Muffie, and she loved us. She was already sleeping on our beds. She knew I was the mommy, and my husband was the daddy. She knew she had to protect our daughter. She became my other baby despite the pound of hair she shed daily. We just kept hoping the good doctor was wrong. But after three months passed, and the dog tipped the scales at 55 pounds, we let loose the final strand of hope. Our Miss Muffie had turned into a German shepherd with a wolf bark that to this day prevents the mailman and any other delivery person from setting foot on our property. They just drop the packages on the lawn and run.

Oh, one other thing about Miss Muffie. She is extremely tall -- about five feet five inches on her hind legs. This trait we're sure is the beagle in her. This has on occasion has posed a problem for us. For example, during dinner Miss Muffie likes to sit under the table. Unfortunately, her tail doesn't always follow her, and it tends to hook on to the bowls and plates on top of the table. The chain reaction is staggering as glass and food go flying all over the place. Perhaps the most serious situation caused by her height occurred when we were visiting my in-laws in upstate New York. Their house is wired with an alarm system that most maximum-security prisons would envy. It seems the dog is too tall for the motion detector. We learned this the hard way when the sirens went off, and six Albany police officers surrounded the house and attempted to break in with guns drawn. I don't think we need to detail out the fiasco which then ensued. The officers turned out to be pretty nice once they secured the premises. They understood of everything except why the monster pooch they called "Cujo" answered to the name "Miss Muffie". But her hot pink collar convinced them that she was not a career criminal, but a nice dog that happened to be in the wrong place at the wrong time. With our assurance that we were only visiting for a short while, the police bade us goodbye.

After that ordeal was over, my lovable lunk of a dog stuck to my side like glue. She slept next to me that night and made me hold her paw. My poor little 85-pound baby was so frightened by the day's events.

I guess when it comes down to it, my sister did pick out a great dog. No matter how big she is, she's still our baby puppy, and we'll love her forever. We're sick that way.

Food For Thought

I was in the pet store the other day looking for a birthday present for my dog. I was pawing over a display of gourmet treats when the owner of the store came to offer assistance. He gently cradled a cat in his arms, but that didn't hinder him from picking up one of the gourmet treat bags and shaking it in my face.

"These are excellent tasting," he said enthusiastically. "All the dogs like them."

Being the cynic I am, I am always skeptical of anyone who tells me how delicious dog food is. What do they do, eat it?

Well, guess what? This guy did. Right there in front of me, he opened a bag of cookie-coated doggie treats and scarfed them down.

"See, they look and taste just like people sugar cookies."

I just stood in stunned silence. He must have sensed my disgust because he immediately began to read off the ingredients on the label to prove to me that nothing in that bag was harmful to humans.

Now, it didn't matter to me that these treats looked like people sugar cookies. And it didn't matter to me what ingredients were in the treats. There could have been double fudge brownies with cheesecake centers in that bag, and I still wouldn't have eaten from it. Why? Because plain as day, on the label, were the words, "DOG FOOD". There was no mention of human beings anywhere. And frankly, I think that's an important distinction. If it was really okay for people to eat this stuff, the bag would have had not only a picture of a dog salivating on it but also a picture of a human being drooling as well. And here's another thought: If it's really okay to eat dog food, then why isn't it sitting on the same shelves as the people food in the big supermarkets?

I tried to explain this to the owner, but he didn't seem to understand. He glared at me suspiciously and pulled his pet cat close to his chest as if he were protecting her from me. I bit my tongue because I almost blurted out,

"I may not like dog food, but I'm a big fan of cat meat."

I tried to figure out why this whole event irked me. It took some time, but then it hit me. This man made me feel like an animal hater because I wouldn't eat the dog food. I don't remember him giving me a pat on the back when I asked if he carried doggie seat belts for the car. And I don't remember him telling me what a good pet owner I was when I purchased expensive doggie shampoo at $8.95 per bottle. I don't spend half that amount on my shampoo. But for my dog, I spent it. And what about the tartar control raw hides I buy my pooch regularly. Does he compliment me on those? No. But because I didn't taste the dog food, he glared at me as if I were wearing a mink coat at an anti-fur rally.

I have to admit, this guy had me feeling guilty. About why I don't know, but I felt as if I had done dogs everywhere a grave disservice. When you think about it, they eat our food. I often sneak my dog a taste of people food. She doesn't seem to mind that. Now, I have to sit and wonder. As she eats this food is she saying, "Wow, I love broiled breast of chicken. Yum-yum!" Or is she really saying, "Yuk, what does she think she's doing, giving me this crud! I'm not a human. I'm going to report her to the Humane Society!"

I think what else made me uneasy about the incident is that this man now thinks I'm close minded and unadventurous when it comes to food. And anyone who knows me knows that is not the case. So, I won't eat doggie biscuits, but I do eat sushi and that's pretty adventurous. Granted, eating raw seafood may not be as smart as eating dog biscuits, but it's my right to be stupid about what I eat and not be judged for my stupidity. That's why it's a free country. You know, I would like to see this man visit one of those countries where they regard chocolate-covered ants as a delicacy. It would be rather interesting to see if he takes part in that little food fest.

Honor Thy Dryer

A few months ago, I experienced a trauma that I wouldn't wish on any other person: my clothes dryer blew up. It didn't literally explode, but there was a bit of smoke, an aroma of burning rubber, a weird, clunky noise and then -- nothing. I knew immediately this was not a good sign So, I called the repair company, and a sympathetic receptionist dispatched a serviceman to my location immediately. So far, I assumed, this mishap seemed controllable.

"Thank Goodness you could be here so fast," I said to the repairman as he took apart my dryer. "I don't know what I'd do without this thing."

"Well, Ma'am, "he said apologetically. "You're going to find out. I have to order a part, and it will take three or four days to come in. Your only other choice is to buy a new dryer."

"What could be so wrong that you can't fix it now?" I asked in disbelief.

"Well, see this rubber part here, it's torn in three pieces," he explained in carefully chosen words. "This usually happens when someone repeatedly overloads the machine."

I knew it. He was blaming me. I predicted this would somehow turn out to be my fault. Immediately, a colorful list of expletives ran through my brain. But what I said was,

"You're sure it will be fixed in three days?"

"Four -- tops," the repairman smiled reassuringly. "I'll order the part as soon as I get back to the shop. It won't be so bad, and it's a lot cheaper to fix the machine than to buy a new one."

After hearing such encouraging words from the repairman, I knew I could weather this storm.

"So for three days, "I told myself, "I won't do laundry. It will be like a vacation."

A week after the repairman's visit, I got a call from the same sympathetic receptionist explaining that the part was on backorder and was not expected to arrive for another two to three weeks.

"We'll just hang a line in back, and dry the clothes the old-fashioned way," my husband said nonchalantly as if he was going to take an active part in this ritual.

"You want me to hang our underwear out in public?"

"It's not going to be hanging from a flagpole. It's in our yard. No one will notice."

I didn't buy that for a moment. I can't tell you how many times I've driven through neighborhoods and observed the size and color of people's underwear hanging outdoors. Now, people were going to do the same thing to me. I couldn't take it. I seriously considered going out and buying a three week supply of new underwear, but I realized that by the time I got through that expense, I could pay for a new dryer. There was no way out. The public hanging had to begin.

So, I bought clothespins at a nearby dollar store. I didn't even know they made them anymore. My husband rigged up a line, and each morning for two weeks, I hung out clothes. I felt like a pioneer woman hanging out my clothes in the crisp, prairie wind. Okay, so my imagination may have wandered a bit, but it got me through this episode.

Then the strangest thing happened. I discovered fabric softener, and my sheets had this great feel to them, and I became hooked on this whole process of air drying! Hanging out the clothes was like meditation for me. It was peaceful; It was wonderful -- until the thunderstorms hit, and I wasn't at home to bring in my spring-fresh wardrobe from outside. I can't tell you how embarrassing it was to stumble into my neighbor's yard to claim my bras which flew across the fence thanks to the overpowering force of Mother Nature and the cheap clothespins from the dollar store!

That one incident was enough to snap me out of my domestic bliss. From then on, I vowed that I would hang my clothes across my living room before I would hang them outside again.

Luckily, the day after the rain incident, I got the call I was waiting for. My dryer part was in. Within minutes, the repairman was at my house hooking up my much-missed appliance.

That night, as I sat in the family room sipping a cup of international coffee and listening to the melodic hum of my dryer emanating from the laundry room, I felt a sense of calm. I still don't understand it. I have lived without a dishwasher and not cared at all. And I know I could live without a television set or a microwave. But touch any appliance that eases the chore of laundry, and it's nothing short of torture. Well, that's not true. If anyone would like to take my iron and hide it so I never,

ever have to press clothes again, feel free. I think I can live with wrinkles and if not, that's why God made dry cleaners.

Explorers Send My Own Mind Wandering

A few weeks ago, my daughter, Coleen, learned about the great explorers in school. For days, my husband and I reacquainted ourselves with the voyages of Christopher Columbus, Henry Hudson and Giovanni da Verrazzano. Even now, I find these explorers fascinating. I know that's not a politically correct thing to say. I know we're not supposed to sing the praises of these brave hearted men who came to the new world in search of gold and other treasures and wound up conquering everyone. But tough, I like these guys. They had guts, and I think we should all be allowed to marvel at their fearless ability to trade in their comfortable landlocked homes for some stark digs on rickety ships which held more rodents than people. And it's not like these voyages were little jaunts across a familiar lake. These guys lived on boats in the middle of the ocean for months -- sometimes years. And these ships had no live shows, no gambling casinos, and no 24-hour buffets. No, these ships provided nothing except vermin, disease and a good case of claustrophobia. But yet, the explorers prevailed.

One explorer I admire greatly is Ferdinand Magellan. The man sailed around the world without the benefit of radar, the Coast Guard or even a tourist information center. He had to wing everything. He chartered his course using nothing more than his wits and the stars. I can't imagine how he did this. I know I couldn't have done it. I can't identify all the major star constellations. On some days, I have trouble identifying the moon. I don't know which way is north, south, east or west. I can barely find my way around the block.

But Magellan and his crew could. They made it all the way around the globe. Okay, I could be cynical here and say, "How do we know he did this?"

Maybe he and his crew went out to sea, stopped off at a few islands, picked up a few souvenirs and waited. Then after a year or so, they headed back to Europe saying they circumnavigated the globe. Who was going to challenge them? I don't think there was any kind of verification committee back then.

When it comes down to it though, I do believe Magellan. He had a goal -- a plan to open up new sea routes for European merchants. He had a tangible idea. This is more than we can say about history's most delusional and lovable explorer, Ponce de Leon.

Poor, poor Ponce. This man was the dreamer of all dreamers. Somewhere, somehow he got the idea that there existed a Fountain of Youth which would make all people virtually immortal. And for some reason, he believed that this Fountain of Youth sat in Florida. How ironic that this man searched the globe and decided that the site of eternal youth, rested on the very same spot that would someday house the world's oldest population.

Personally, I think Ponce was the victim of one of the most successful and elaborate practical jokes ever played on a human being. No one else would fall for such a scheme except for of course, the stupid monarch who funded this foolish quest. I think if I got to talk to Ponce de Leon, I would have to ask how he found out about this fountain. Who could have started this rumor? I'm beginning to think it was his wife who just wanted him out of the house for a year or two.

"Ponce, will you travel across the sea and find me some of that youth water?" she probably asked in a flirtatious manner. "Think of how much fun we could have if I remained young and beautiful forever."

I think that's all Ponce had to hear and he was off hiring a crew. For us, 400 years later, it's easy to assume that Ponce de Leon may have been a bit naive and made a few errors in judgment. After all, we have modern science to tell us there is no fountain of youth. We all know, unlike Ponce, that eternal youth does not come from a fountain. Today, we all know eternal youth comes from a wrinkle cream jar or a board certified plastic surgeon. Hm. What was I saying about foolish quests?

Taking Flack over My Christmas tree

About the first week of December every year, my husband, daughter and I embark on our annual Christmas tree hunt. I know what you're all thinking. Here's a family that honors a sentimental Christmas tradition which exemplifies the meaning of this special holiday. They go as a family to find their special tree.

Well, I'm sorry to say this, but you're wrong. My family does nothing special to find our tree. We don't go to tree farms. We don't take day-long trips into the mountains, and we don't visit every Christmas tree lot in the tri-state area in search of the perfect fir. No. Our plan is simple. We look through the circulars of the big home hardware stores, and the first store to advertise trees is the first store we go to. On the average, it takes us about two minutes to decide on a suitable tree. That's about the time we need to pinch some needles and wiggle a few branches. Our family record for finding a tree is 90 seconds.

I know that to all the old-fashioned Christmas people out there, we sound like a family of Scrooges. But I have to say, I like this fast-paced tradition. I have no desire to drag myself or my family through a muddy tree farm to cut down my own tree. It's a tree. I'm going to throw it out two weeks after I put it up. Frankly, I feel guilty about that as it is. I know that I'm responsible for the demise of this tree, and I don't want to witness it happening.

Probably, when it comes down to it, we are the perfect family for an artificial tree, but I can't bring myself to go that route either. I love the smell of the pine in my living room. I even like the needles when they fall on the floor. They get sucked up in the vacuum cleaner and I get that pine scent in my house for months after the holidays.

In our defense, I want to say that we're not complete Christmas tree poopers. While we spend little time on obtaining the tree, we do put a great deal of effort into decorating it. Over the years, we have collected special ornaments that adorn our not so special tree. Every time we unwrap our ornaments, a rush of sentiment overtakes me. Our tree is best described as a hodgepodge of memories thrown together in a totally unplanned and impulsive fashion. We have modern ornaments, antique ornaments, elegant ornaments and tacky ornaments. And I love each one of these treasures. I wouldn't part with anyone of them because they say a little bit about the kind of family we are.

Some of our friends scoff at our tree. They say it's too eclectic. They don't like eclectic. Many of them prefer to do theme trees. One year, a friend went completely Victorian and bought all new ornaments to fit that theme. The next year, she had become sick of the Victorian period and went Disney instead. Of course, this meant that she had to invest in all new Disney ornaments. I was impressed. This is quite and expensive undertaking. If I did that, I would have nothing left over to buy gifts. And to be perfectly honest, I see no reason to blow all my money on ornaments that sit in a box in my attic for 11 1/2 months out of the year.

Over the years, I have also noticed that some people have turned into Christmas tree snobs. They believe in a tree caste system, and they will tell you boldly to your face if you bought an inferior fir.

"Oh, that's a Canadian Balsam isn't it? Anyone who knows Christmas trees knows that the Douglas Fir is the Cadillac of trees."

My question to them is always "Who died and made you King of the Christmas tree forest?"

They usually just shake their heads at me in pity. But tough on them. If I want to have a blue spruce or a scotch pine sitting in my living room, I will. And I shouldn't have to take criticism for it especially -- and again I bring up this point -- that in two weeks it won't matter. For even the Cadillac of all trees will be sitting on the curb waiting for the trash men to come and take it away.

Despite my fussing and complaining over the tradition of Christmas trees, I do have to concede one thing. The tree -- be it artificial or straight from the forest -- brings a sense of hope into my home. I'm sure that hope is present all the time. I just let it get lost in the stresses of day to day life. Although I may not always get the perfect tree or the best fir, I don't care. I know why that tree is there, and so does my family. And that's our tradition.

This Spring, I'll Rough It at the Four Seasons

Well, it's spring again. The winter doldrums have passed, and it seems as if the whole world is ready to face the magic that only the newness of spring has to offer. For some people, the season of spring ushers in feelings of joy and excitement. For others, spring is synonymous with getting back to nature and our earthly roots. And on behalf of myself and my family, I can honestly say that spring holds for us special meaning as well. For us, spring means spending five days in a big city, luxury hotel room that boasts a Jacuzzi, at least 100 cable channels and 24-hour-a-day room service.

Now, before you all judge me to be a selfish and materialistic person, let me explain how I came to associate the resurgence of spring with a vacation of opulence and laziness. When we were first married, my husband and I embarked on a springtime camping trip with newly-made friends to some mountains somewhere in the middle of Pennsylvania. From this adventure, I learned two things: I will never go away with people I hardly know, and I will always bring my own car in case I need to escape. Initially, the camping trip sounded like a wonderfully romantic idea. I envisioned campfires, hot cocoa and the sounds of Mother Nature lulling us to sleep. I wasn't afraid of camping. After all, I did it with the Girl Scouts some 10 years before and I don't mean to brag, but I got a badge for it. Granted, we didn't stay overnight, and we didn't build a fire, and we brought tons of food and drink. But technically, it was camping: there were trees and dirt.

But from the outset, this camping trip with our friends had a different air about it. I had gone out and purchased the most fashionable of camping clothes and accessories for me and my husband. I bought flannel shirts, lanterns, a Swiss army knife and a compass. You name it, I got it -- except for a tent. For some reason, I assumed that we were going to stay in one of those neat campers that can be hooked up to electricity and water. Apparently, I assumed wrong. These friends didn't believe in campers. No, they believed in sleeping on the ground under the stars with wild animals and insects. To them, camping wasn't camping unless you looked Mother Nature in the eye and devoured it. For us, camping conjured up images of peace and tranquility. To them, camping was a survival weekend that most Marines couldn't live through.

And it wasn't just the sleeping arrangements that alarmed me. Our fellow vacationers brought no food. They believed in foraging and fishing for their meals, and they wanted us to do the same. Luckily for us, I go nowhere without rations. I packed hot dogs; I packed popcorn; and I packed Twinkies.

Only five hours into this trip, I realized something else: there were no bathrooms. Aside from the problem of where I was going to plug in my blow dryer, there was this little issue about where the commode was.

"You want a bathroom? There is your bathroom," sneered one friend as she gestured toward the forest. "Go into the woods -- anywhere in the woods."

"Oh, I don't think so," I responded in utter disbelief. "I'm really an indoor bathroom person. I need porcelain."

"We're living in nature now. We go by nature's rules."

"No, I go by my mother's rules, and my mother has always insisted I use a toilet. It's one of her quirks."

I realized then that we were in over our heads with these people, but I knew if we just made it through the next few days, we would never have to speak to them again. We just had to act polite now, so they wouldn't abandon us in this God forsaken wilderness. And this thought gave me the strength to go on. I have to admit outside of camping, this couple was warm, friendly and smart. And if I had to be stranded in the woods with any two people, I would choose them.

But they didn't care about plumbing, and plumbing is a big part of my life. Needless to say, we survived. My husband and I cuddled as we slept on the ground in sleeping bags, but I never closed my eyes. For three days, I imagined that fuzzy spiders, skunks and snakes were trying to make their way into my sleeping bag. And those sounds of nature that I thought would be so comforting -- well, I found they can do a really good job of scaring the heck out of even the most rational of people.

Anyway, it's this experience that pushed me into my current practice of high-priced spring getaways. I know most people don't approve of how I choose to spend my vacations. Even my husband has a tough time with it. Every year, he asks if we can find some compromise between the horrors of outdoor camping and the enormous costs of a four-star hotel.

"Why can't we stay in a motel? You would like it," he tries to convince me. "They have ice and snack machines. And most motels have real bathrooms."

"No, I want people to be at my beck and call," I argue back. "We work hard all year. I want to have luxury, maid service and a real closet to hang my clothes."

I have to admit that one year, I came close to giving in and trying a new type of vacation. Another of my well-meaning friends almost convinced me to spend our spring vacation with them in a condominium in Florida. I thought the idea of a home away from home sounded cozy and comfortable. But then as I listened to my friend describe how our vacation would be, a wave of panic swept over me. She wanted us to cook all our meals in the condo every day in order to save a few dollars. There would be no maid service or truffles on our pillows. We would have to make beds, pick up dishes, and yes, share a bathroom. The red warning flag sprung up and danced feverishly in front of my eyes. This wasn't going to be a vacation; this was everyday life -- just transported to another state! I jumped out of that vacation faster than I would jump out of a burning building.

I know the perfect vacation differs from person to person. And to be truthful, I still hold out hope that one day I will want to return to the woods and experience the serenity and joy that Mother Nature has to offer. I know that springtime in the country can be an eye awakening experience, but from what I understand springtime in Paris is nothing to scoff at either. Hopefully, one day I can check it out and let you know.

I Glue Now Where I Used to Sew

It used to be in my house that when a hem came down on a skirt, it would wind up first in the sewing pile and eventually in the old clothes pile. In truth, these piles are one in the same because I can't sew. It's not that I can't sew curtains or dresses. I can't sew a stitch. I've tried, but I'm just no good at it.

When I was a teenager, my mother suggested I take a nine-week sewing course which my high school offered. I went to a prep school, and in those four years of prep school, this is the one and only course I almost had to take over in the summer. It was horrible. While my classmates sewed these wonderful outfits during this two-and-a-half-month stint, I sewed a vest. It was only through tearful negotiation that I pulled out a C- . My teacher said she'd pass me if I promised to avoid two career choices: seamstress and surgeon.

Laugh if you will, but for my mother, the woman who can probably sew together a car, this was a disgrace from which she almost never recovered. My sisters sewed. Although in fairness, one of them was only a tad more talented at this endeavor than me. My grandmothers sewed. My aunts sewed. My cousins sewed. I was the black sheep of the family. So, in true spirit, I tried to prove myself. I attempted to repair the hem of my coat, and in doing so, I sewed it to the living room sofa. After that incident, the rule was set down. I was not allowed to hold a needle and thread again.

Unfortunately, my reputation for sewing has carried over into my married life. My husband sews on the buttons on his shirts after he rejected my policy which stated,

"If it loses a button, it's a rag."

My daughter keeps her own sewing pile. She waits for my mother to come to visit, and then she hits her with all her needed repairs.

This was until I purchased my glue gun.

To whoever invented this magical appliance, I say this: I owe you my life. Glue guns fix everything. They hem; they bond; they cement; they do it all. I now keep my glue gun on my kitchen counter next to my electric can opener. It's ready to go at a moment's notice.

My friends find this a bit odd, and they have been known to scoff at me. But it was I who had the last laugh when they wasted hours sewing Brownie badges on their daughters' girl scout sashes, and I did mine in seconds with my trusty glue gun. When they saw what I had done, they let out a collective,

"Good idea. I never would have thought about that."

In the last two years, glue guns have been improved. I now have the super duper model from Sears which had an assortment of glue cartridges. My gun came in this nifty case with a map of a house which displayed which cartridge was best to use in each room. For example, if I break a dish in the kitchen, I use #200. If I need to glue silk flowers on to a wreath for my front door, I use #100. Nothing is simpler.

I think the next models should have even more useful applications. How about first-aid? Imagine using the glue gun to fix lacerations. No more stitches. Why not? The gun is heated, so it's sanitary. The glue is never re-used, and eventually it would wear off after the cut is healed..

How about edible glue? Your two-layer cake falls apart. With an edible, colorful glue cartridge, you can sew that cake right back together, and no one will know you goofed up.

While my husband is thrilled I found this handy tool, he does think I go too far with it. When we did our taxes, and the instructions said to fasten all papers together, he got upset because I wanted to use the glue gun. I couldn't find the stapler, and I didn't think the IRS would mind. But he did.

I know in this age of computers and lasers and medical breakthroughs, it seems silly to be so excited over something as simple as my glue gun. And yes, I rely heavily on all that computer wizardry and the assorted Star Trek-type products that come from that technology. But it's like the glue gun was meant for me.

Sometimes, as I'm using this wonderful invention, I think about the person or persons who brainstormed this idea, and I wonder what they are up to now. Is there a new product of this magnitude on the horizon? Are these inventors open for suggestions? If so, I have some ideas that would benefit me and I'm sure a lot of people greatly.

For instance, we could all use a product that automatically recharges the light bulbs on top of stairwells so that we wouldn't have to endanger our lives climbing up extension ladders. It hurts a lot when one falls off those ladders. Secondly, we need pots and pans whose bottoms don't burn up if someone forgets they've been on the stove with nothing in them for more than an hour. And lastly, and most importantly, we need a clothes dryer that will sort, fold and iron all laundry into coordinating outfits.

I know you are all thinking that I'm asking too much. But I'm sure somewhere along the line someone said to herself;

"Gee, I wish there was a glue apparatus that would take care of all my sewing and cementing needs."

And look what happened with that.

When Grandchildren Come to Visit

I recently read an article which talked about appropriate precautions grandparents should take when their grandchildren come to visit. I knew this was what the article was supposed to be about because that's what the headline said it was about. Had I failed to read that headline beforehand, I'm sure I would have thought I was reading the national security plan for a surprise nuclear missile attack. As I read this article, my only thought was, "This is one scared Grandpa."

There's no denying kids can be wild. There's no denying kids can be mischievous. But this guy suggested that grandparents photograph and record the serial numbers of all valuables, and then lock these valuables away in a fireproof safe. Again, the question ran through my mind, "What kind of grandchildren does this guy have? Are they trained terrorists?"

It's safe to say that most grandchildren are not terrorists. But, in truth and fairness, I must say that the writer of this article made a valid point. Children tend to think that Grandma and Grandpa's house is a place where all the regular rules of decorum do not apply. Why kids get this idea is a mystery, but it may have something to do with the fact that grandparents and grandchildren know that visits don't last forever. So, both parties cut loose a bit, enjoy the moment and estimate the damage the morning after.

One way to minimize that damage is to avoid boredom -- not only for the grandchildren but for the grandparents. For instance, it's probably not a good idea to make grandchildren watch anything on television that is in black and white. The only exceptions for this are shows like *The Munsters* or *The Addams Family*. Never expect an eight-year-old to watch a World War II movie about D-day or the Battle of the Bulge. Most eight-year-olds never even heard of The Battle of the Bulge unless they saw it on a Weight Watchers commercial. If an eight-year-old wants to watch a World War II movie, then watch out. Maybe he or she is a trained terrorist. On the flip side of that coin, grandchildren should not force grandparents to watch hours of programming like MTV. Music video shows usually do not bond grandparents to grandchildren. These shows scare grandparents. They see the clothes, the hair, the tattoos, the multiple-body piercings, and they think

"Wow, we thought we had it bad with our kids in the 60's. That was a piece of cake next to this generation."

Probably, the best rule of thumb to follow is avoid television completely. Some experts suggest that grandparents keep a strict schedule of activities when grandchildren visit. These should be activities that both grandparent and grandchild enjoy such as a trip to the zoo, a walk in the park, art projects or maybe even gardening. There is one caveat to the schedule theory: allow some flexibility. Remember, visiting a grandparent should be fun and educational. What it should not be is boot camp.

Of course, all the planning in the world isn't going to help if your grandchildren's visit turns into a permanent arrangement. This is not an uncommon occurrence. It's known as the Boomerang Effect. Grown children move out, start families, and return home to live with their aging parents and surprise -- they bring their own children with them.

While some grandparents enjoy the Boomerang Effect, others fear it. Why? Because grown children returning home with their kids deny the older generation the joy of getting depressed over the Empty Nest Syndrome. With the children and grandchildren all under one roof, how can the older parent make their children feel guilty for never visiting them in their golden years? It's impossible, and the human tradition of guilt and neglect is lost to that generation forever.

Since no one can predict what the future holds, grandparents have to be prepared. If the grandchildren come for a visit, let them know that rules do exist in the house. That doesn't mean you can't spoil them. That's a grandparent's right. But if a few weeks go by, and you notice that your children and grandchildren have made no attempt to leave, cut back on the permissive attitude. You may be making it too hard for them to leave. If a month goes by, and they still aren't packing, watch out! Your empty nest dreams may be ready to fly the coop.

Three Cents Shakes the Sense out of Supermarket Shoppers

I ran to the store to get some decaffeinated coffee. Usually when I go into a store with the intention of buying one thing, I come out with a cart full of merchandise. But on this day, I was expecting my parents and sister for a visit, so I had to hurry home. I picked out my coffee and briskly walked to the express lane proud that I had defeated all temptation to shop.

"Not too bad," I thought to myself as I sized up the crowd at the check out counter. "Only one person in front of me and the line forming behind me. What great timing! I'll be out in seconds."

This optimistic thought didn't even have time to completely exit my brain before it burst into a million different pieces. The woman in front of me, a woman who obviously had too much time on her hands, seized the moment to start a fight with the cashier over the price of a dozen eggs. Apparently, her eggs rang up three cents higher than the price she thought they should be. Initially, I silently sided with this woman who I viewed as a crusader for consumer rights. But as precious seconds ticked away, and the demands of this woman turned from noble to ridiculous, I found myself seeing this irate shopper not so much as Ralph Nader but as Leona Helmsley with a bad attitude. I was clearly becoming annoyed.

What steered me on my path to impatience was the woman's insistence that her whole order be voided so that the cashier could re-enter each item as she watched. The poor kid admitted the eggs rang up incorrectly, but that wasn't good enough. No, she had convinced herself that this young man was making a conscious effort to rip her off, and she wanted to catch him at it.

"Ma'am, I'll have to send for the manager to void the order."

"Fine!" she said testily. "Get the manager. I'll wait."

Before I could say, "Take three cents from me, please don't make him send for the manager", the nervous cashier flipped on the light over his register and stopped all activity on his line.

I felt panic for I knew that little light flashing over the register meant at least a 10-minute delay because supermarket managers always take ten minutes to get to their cashiers in trouble. I think it's some kind of grocery store rule. I also knew I didn't have ten minutes to spare. My parents would be arriving any minute. No one would be home. My mother would be waiting in the car outside my house concluding one of two things: either I forgot all about them and their two-hour trek down to see me; or worse, I slipped, fell in the house and lay injured and unable to call out for help. My nervousness grew by the second. I began to feel the weight of the future guilt I was going to experience for worrying my mother.

I was losing control. Desperately, I scanned the other check out stations hoping to see an empty aisle. But there was none. Even if one opened, I couldn't get to it. The line behind me had grown to more than 10 people. There was no way I could jump over 10 people and beat them to a shorter line. They held a better position, and I was trapped.

After I performed a few seconds of deep-breathing exercises, the manager arrived and asked what the problem was all about. Before the instigating female could answer, I chimed in ever so calmly,

"You have a whacko woman and a hundred people waiting on your express line because of three lousy cents. Fix this now!"

The old man behind me applauded. He called the woman an inconsiderate troublemaker. He accused her of putting more than 15 items on the conveyor belt. The rest of the express line cheered him on. For one brief moment, I felt a pang of sympathy for this woman until she yelled back at the old man.

"Three cents is three cents! I want my three cents!"

Then all hell broke loose. It was a mess.

And while all this went on, the cashier frantically rang up the woman's order again. As quickly as he could, he threw her groceries into three plastic bags, and gave her back change for a $100 bill -- plus three extra cents. Content with her victory, the thrifty rabble rouser turned and gave us all a grunt of indignation. Then she went on her merry way. Since I only had to pay for my decaf coffee, I caught up with the woman at the exit doors. My first instinct was to blast her again, but deep within me, I heard a voice guiding me toward right action, "Let it go, Let it go."

And I followed that advice -- for a moment -- until I saw her climb into a brand new Cadillac which, by the way, was parked in the fire lane in front of the store.

Then my little voice turned into a big yell, and it screamed to her across the crowded parking lot,

"You should be ashamed of yourself acting that way for three lousy cents! And you're parked illegally. How selfish can you possibly be?"

She hurried into her car and sped off embarrassed that I had made a scene. Was this the wisest move on my part? Probably not, and I must admit I regretted my actions later. But I did learn from this experience. I know now I need to develop more tolerance for people -- no matter their faults. I know I need to calm down and take things more in stride. And I know, and so should this woman, that it's a damn good thing for her I drink mainly decaf. Could you imagine me, caffeine and her -- all waiting on the same line.

Holidays - Bah! Humbug!

I was out with my friend Mary the other day, and she began to tell me about her husband's company social. It is held in the beginning of November, and this gathering takes the place of the former holiday party. Not being a corporate person, I had a tough time understanding why this company felt it couldn't hold a holiday bash during the holiday season. Then, she enlightened me on with the philosophy of political correctness.

It seems that any party in December may be construed as a plot to focus attention on Christmas or Hanukkah. And this is now wrong. Celebrating holidays shows a lack of sensitivity. I missed out. I didn't know that these holidays turned bad. I guess all that joy, peace and love influence people the wrong way. Imagine, people taking the time to be kind to each other. What is this world coming to?

Holiday lovers beware. If Christmas and Hanukkah are on the chopping block, what's next? My guess is Valentine's Day. How can we endorse a holiday whose chief character, a roving angel, shoots arrows filled with love potion at people? Is this romance or is this a felony?

Let's look at recent headlines for the answer. If a six-year-old boy can be accused of sexual harassment for kissing a classmate on the cheek, what kind of chance does a naked cherub with a drugged arrow have? I think the best he can hope for is five to ten in some state penitentiary.

The spring holiday, the one that starts with an E has managed to survive. Socially aware people like to welcome spring as long as it is done in a totally non-religious fashion with tons of bunnies. Even the animal rights groups go along with the "Big E" as long as the exploitation of bunnies and baby chicks is kept to a minimum.

Halloween is the only holiday that has witnessed a surge in popularity. It is now the second most popular holiday in this country. I'm sure there is some great psychological reason why we love to dress up and act like monsters and lunatics. It's probably to relieve the stress we suffer from being sensitive all the time. But that's okay by me. I love Halloween. Fake cemetery stones adorn my front lawn along with spider webs and ghosts.

But I remember a few years back, public opinion started to turn on Halloween. No longer could kids wear costumes like Dracula and Frankenstein to school. It seems their classmates got scared. Well, of course they got scared. It was Halloween. That's the whole point of this holiday. But since the emotional trauma argument won out, every school-age kid has had to settle on being some friendly Disney character or a fairy princess.

Even the symbol of Halloween, the Witch, has met with harsh criticism. It seems real witches object to the old crone image of the Halloween witch because it reinforces a negative stereotype. I guess they're right. After all, I'm sure Glinda the Good Witch of the North would object if she was around.

Perhaps my most memorable yet perplexing view of Halloween came from the parent of a child in my daughter's pre-school class. The day of the class's costume party, she not only scolded me for my enthusiasm for Halloween, but she accused me of giving in to the satanic forces that rule the Earth.

Truthfully, I had a hard time with that one. I don't think I'm a satanic person unless of course I'm going through PMS, but that's another story. For the most part, I don't think there are many satanic people around. I have never met any -- even during my college years when I lived in the Bronx.

Okay, there may have been some unsavory characters, but I don't think they were satanic. My guess is that the truly evil people are few and far between, and they don't need to wait for a holiday like Halloween to reek their havoc on the rest of humanity.

It's plain to see that all holidays can come under fire when we try to accommodate every person in the world at the same time. Frankly, I think the people who have set up all these rigid standards of behavior need to ease up and enjoy life a little more. I think these "sensitive" people who worry about what everyone else thinks should take to heart the words of Frosty the Snowman, you know that fun-loving character from that famous December holiday,

"Chill out or you're going to melt away."

My Home Office

I have a favorite commercial. It goes like this. A woman works from home all day in her robe and bunny slippers. She is connected to the world through her high-tech communication toys. She never takes a shower, she never leaves her house, and she never gets interrupted by anyone or anything that exists outside her home office. Now, I understand this is a commercial. I know it's supposed to extol the virtues of high-tech living. I know it's supposed to show the world that even the most important business deals can be done via phone, fax and computer. But each time I see that commercial, the only words that pop into my head are: What a crock!

Anyone who has ever worked from home knows it isn't what this commercial would have you believe. First of all, the woman in this commercial never receives any other phone calls during the day besides her business phone calls. Where are the office equipment salespeople, the health insurance salespeople, the friends who want to have lunch, and anyone else who just called to chat in the middle of the day because they know that working from home is somehow synonymous with not working at all?

I have to confess, that I was one of those misguided souls who believed that working from home would be a piece of cake. I remember when I made the decision.

"There will be no commuting cost, and I can be home with Coleen," I told myself logically. "I can have a flexible schedule, wear sweat pants every day, and still take care of the things I need to do around the house."

But do you know what I forgot to factor into this arrangement? Guilt. The guilt that comes with knowing that downstairs in the laundry room are at least two piles of clothes waiting to be folded and put away.

"I should fold those clothes," I argue with myself. "No, if I fold those clothes, I miss valuable work time. I should stay here and work." And the debate goes back and forth in my warped brain until my confusion and guilt paralyze me. And to my dismay, my work remains unfinished, and my clothes remain unfolded. The same guilt torments me when I take off to go to the supermarket or -- God forbid -- to go get my hair cut. That is guilt which lasts for days.

I know working from home has its perks. I hear friends talk about office politics, and I must admit, I enjoy not having to deal with that stuff. My own office means I can take off to volunteer at my daughter's school whenever I'm needed. I am free to take my lunch at 11 AM so I can watch the Rosie O'Donnell Show. Working from home also means my dog isn't alone all day. She hangs out with me and keeps me company as I pace, write, edit and curse -- my usual writing routine. And working from home eliminates the awkward decision about whether or not I should go to the company Christmas party. There is no Christmas party unless you count the one day a year I wrap garland around the dog's collar, play Bing Crosby tapes and sip egg nog at my computer.

I think the greatest challenge to a home office is the cabin fever. I work and live in the same rooms every day, and this can be stifling. I have a terrible habit of confronting my husband as soon as he comes in the door.

"Let's go out for dinner or let's go walk in the mall," I shout at him at warp speed before his feet are planted inside the house.

"Can I change my clothes first?" he asks.

"Do you have to? I've been cooped up all day."

"I've just driven 40 miles home. Let me breathe a second. Let me see my family, my dog, my bathroom! "

Unfortunately, this is where trouble begins. Our commuting habits are not compatible. What usually happens is I take off by myself for an hour or so, and he stays home with our daughter and the dog. He revels in the serenity of his home; I escape it.

Do I hate working from home? No. But it's a challenge which requires a lot more than a comfortable robe and a pair of fluffy bunny slippers to make it work.

To Kill a Spider

The last time my husband was away on business, I thought I'd surprise him and clean out his shop in the basement. I made great progress. I cleaned everywhere. I even removed cobwebs that hung from the rafters. I soon learned that this was a mistake for out of nowhere crawled this huge spider. I know this sounds strange, but I think it was mad at me. My guess was that my cleaning destroyed its web, and it wanted me to know about it.

So, I took the only action possible. I looked this arachnid straight in the eye. Then I raised my foot and slammed it down on the floor. I squashed that bug beyond recognition. Sure, I was disgusted by the mess, but it had to be done. I then turned off the light, shut the door and left the remains for my husband. I felt not a pang of remorse .

"You know, you don't have to kill these things," Edward scolded me as he scraped the bug guts off the floor the following evening.. "Spiders eat other bugs. They have a definite purpose."

"Look at the size of that thing!" I argued. "It was as big as a Buick. It should have had airbags. I think it ate more than its fair share of food."

Edward decided not to pursue the conversation. He knows there is no arguing with my personal insect credo, "The only good bug is a dead bug."

Oh, I know how heartless that sounds, but I'm not all bad. If a bug is outside, I let it live. That's its right. But if it invades my house or builds a nest anywhere under my roof, it's dead along with its fellow bug family members.

I know I'm not the only spider hater in the world. There are plenty of people who hate spiders, and just for the record, I'm not talking just women. I know lots of macho men who cringe when they see the eight-legged creatures. I think the problem with spiders is that they are so repulsive looking. If God only made them cute, everyone would think twice about stomping on them. I don't want to tick anybody off, but I think God made a mistake here.

If only He had planned it out better. Look at ladybugs. No one kills ladybugs. Everyone likes them. What about butterflies? People try to catch them on their fingertips. They take pictures of them. They plant flowers to attract these insects. No one takes pictures of spiders. There is nothing appealing about them. The bigger they get, the ickier they get.

I have tried to practice spider tolerance in my house. If I see a little one dangling from a web in the corner of the kitchen ceiling, I try to let it be. I say to myself,

"It's a baby spider. It's not hurting anyone. Let it alone."

But the problem with this is the next day when I go to look for the spider in the same corner, and it's gone. Then, I think,

"Where did it go? Is it in my cupboards with my food? Will I find it in my cereal?"

I know these are irrational thoughts, but there's little I can do about them once I get myself going.

In all fairness, spiders are not the only crawling things that make people sweat. Ants do a good job too. When most people see an ant, they panic. They either call an exterminator immediately, or they buy hundreds of those little traps and place them all over the house. For they know where there is one ant, there are hundreds of ants.

What's really strange about ants is that they can be considered both pests and pets at the same time. People spend hundreds of dollars to rid their homes of these tiny creatures, then these same people turn around and buy ant farms. If humans find this confusing, what do ants think? Don't you think the ants in the farm notice when the people they live with call in the Terminix man to blow their relatives away just because they took a stroll on a kitchen countertop? Talk about your psychological warfare.

Can Denim Bring on Depression?

Last month, I went shopping for a pair of jeans. An easy assignment or so I thought. After all, how hard could it be to go into a store, find a few pairs in my size, try them on, and take one home?

As it turned out, it was really hard. There are a lot of choices that go into buying a pair of jeans. First, I had to decide if I'm a petite, average or tall. Well, at 5'3", I'm officially in the petite category. But, due to some freak, genetic mix-up, I'm built like a tall person. I have long legs and a short waist which means I don't fit into the petite cut jeans. So, I have to buy a longer length which means I have to hem. And I hate to do that especially when it comes to denim.

Next, I had to decide if I wanted to try on the slim, relaxed or misses cut. This is a tough decision if you are unfamiliar with these terms. Here's my translation. Slim cut is for teenagers and naturally thin women who never weigh more than 98 pounds. The relaxed fit is for women who want a bit more room in the waist so they can enjoy a meal and still walk away from the table with the top button of their pants fastened. The misses cut is for women who are experiencing the terror of gravity. The misses cut gives women extra room in the hips, thighs, waist and seat. I don't think I need to go into more detail than that.

I knew enough to bypass the slim cut. So, I took a pair of relaxed fit and average length jeans into the dressing room with me. All three were different brand names. One pair didn't make it past my thighs. The second pair, I could have fit two of me into, and the third had enough leg length for Shaquille O'Neal.

So, I took them out and tried three more pair. I mixed and matched cuts and sizes. This went on for an hour. What I found was that the size on the tag is irrelevant in women's jeans. Each company has its own criteria for determining a size. I can fit into one label's size 8 and another's size 12. One minute, I'm having the thinnest day of my life, and the next minute I'm buying two canisters of Ultra-Slim Fast and a treadmill.

I'm not a person who walks around with blinders on. It's been a couple of years since I bought new jeans, so I may have put on a few pounds. I can't say for sure. I banished my bathroom scale sometime ago. Even if I have gone up a size, I should be able to go and buy the next size. I can accept a size 8 or a size 10 if that is what I am. But I don't think jeans designers should play with my mind. That's just downright cruel.

My friends tell me that the "floating size" problem exists in all types of fashion, and it's getting worse. If this is the case, it could pose a major problem especially when it comes to gift buying. For example, my husband counts on me to tell him what size I am before he does his holiday shopping. He goes, he buys, I try on, it fits-- we're all happy. But if a size differs from designer to designer, then he has to guess which size looks like it would fit me. For a husband, this could be dangerous. What if he thinks the size 12 looks like me. In his mind, he knows I told him I'm a size 8 or 10. Should he take the chance, buy me that outfit and hope that it's too big on me? Or worse, should he buy me that outfit in a smaller size, and wait for all hell to break loose when I discover it's too tight, and I can't get the zipper up? Tough call to make.

There may be a bright side to all of this. If my husband becomes anxious guessing my correct clothing size, he may have to resort to buying gifts where a bigger size is more appreciated. For instance: gemstones. With diamonds or emeralds, the larger the size, the bigger the smile. On second thought, maybe this size thing does have some advantages.

Home Demonstrations Can Add Intrigue to Daily Life

A few weeks ago, I attended a kitchen utensil demonstration at the home of one of my friends. I know most women say they hate these demonstrations, but I'm not one of them. I was happy to be included. I had heard only good things about this culinary company's cooking tools, and I was eager to see them in use. And this demonstration did not disappoint me. There were gadgets for every kind of kitchen chore imaginable. I admit I didn't even recognize some of these gadgets until the ever chirpy saleswoman demonstrated their use. There were new and improved cheese graters, ice cream scoopers, apple parers, garlic presses, baking stones.... you name it, this demonstration had it. It was a gourmet's dream.

Unfortunately, these days, I am mostly a fast food restaurant's dream; so, many of these gadgets were lost on me. But I appreciated their purpose, and to prove this, I purchased $40 worth of merchandise. Will I use what I bought? Well, probably not. But that night I was so sure I was going to use everything. I didn't want to cook when I left that demonstration; I wanted to create. I wanted to be the next Julia Child. But alas, I knew that feeling would be short lived. I knew that feeling would dissipate the moment I pulled into my driveway.

You might ask then, "Why did you buy the stuff?"

The answer is simple: everyone else did. Yes, I fell victim to peer pressure. I didn't want anyone to think I was a dweeb because I didn't know how to use all that paraphernalia. The women at this demonstration really knew their tools. They "oohed " and "aahed" over the two-in- one salt and pepper shaker. They drooled over the stain-resistant ladles. They couldn't wait to get their hands on the garlic press that was so much more efficient than the ones they had at home.

After witnessing all this, what was I going to say?

"I don't have a garlic press. I've always been a big believer in garlic powder."

No, that wouldn't fly -- not in this room. These women knew that the right tools could make a good cook a great cook. I was definitely out of my league.

If I think back on it, the hottest item that evening was the combination parer and corer which could skin, core and slice apples, potatoes and a variety of other fruits and vegetables into little ringlets within seconds.

"Won't that make baking pies so easy?" one woman whispered to me. "Do you bake pies?"

"Do Mrs. Smith's pies count?" I answered jokingly.

"You don't bake even during the holidays?"

"No," I answered honestly. "I have sisters and sisters-in-law who do it so well. I just let them have all the fun. Besides, I've tried to bake, and it's not a pleasant sight."

That woman didn't turn around and talk to me anymore after I confided to her about my lack of baking skill. But I did score points with the saleswoman when she found out I owned the granddaddy of all baking stones -- a 15-inch round stone that can make enough pizza for 12 people. Even the most experienced cooks in that room were impressed with me. I, of course, didn't admit that I never use the stone because it's too heavy to lift out of drawer where it's stored.

Although this demonstration was unique in the products that were sold, it was amazingly similar to the other demonstrations I've been invited to over the past year or so. Let's see. I've been asked to several candle demonstrations, a gift basket demonstration, a make up demonstration, a rubber stamp demonstration and a psychic demonstration which to this day still gives me the creeps. I'll go to any demonstration. I love them. I may not go crazy over the products, but it's a night out. There is usually food, and a lot of laughing and talking with friends. And if I can contain my impulse to spend, it can be an economical night out as well.

I know a lot of women dread getting an invitation to a demonstration in the mail. They view it with fear. They become intimidated by the idea that they may have to participate in a new activity that they've never tried before. I understand this is frightening. I, for one, turned down the opportunity to use the extra sharp paring knife at the kitchen demonstration. I have learned the hard way, that any object that's guaranteed to remain razor blade sharp for life should not be in my possession. On the other hand, I had great fun learning at the psychic demonstration that in a supposed earlier life, my daughter was actually my mother. Personally, I thought that this little tidbit of information shed a great deal of light on our relationship. Is it true? Who knows? But I'll keep it in mind. It may come in handy when my daughter approaches those wicked teenage years.

Ladies Night Out

Once every two months, I and four friends, embark on our own low-key, mental health adventure which usually involves a movie and cholesterol-laden snacks. For simplicity reasons, we refer to this event as "Ladies Night Out". However, in truth, it should be called "Get us out of our houses now before we kill someone" night!

I'm sure there are many women out there who feel the need to abandon their responsibilities for one evening and just let loose. For all of you who have experienced these cravings of escape, but don't know how to fulfill them, let me give you some advice.

1. Give Family Advance Notice. This is the first rule to follow. Kids need time to absorb the fact that Mom won't be home to cook dinner, supervise baths or read bedtime stories. Dads need the time to make arrangements for food, come up with creative ways to skip the baths and figure out what two videos will keep the kids busy while he watches the hockey game or any other sporting event broadcast on any of the 98 different cable channels. If you are in a situation where Dad is not available to supervise the children, you will need time to find a sitter who is willing to endure the abuse that your children will heap on him or her in those four hours that you are gone. This is not an easy task. Most sitters need at least a week's notice and a written guarantee that they will not have to change a diaper or clean up vomit.

2. Synchronize your watches with your friends the day before you're scheduled to go out. Also determine who will drive. Remember, punctuality is the key to a successful escape. Some mothers need to tell their children the exact hour and minute they will be leaving. This gives those children a chance to get out all their howling, screaming and crying before Mommy's ride to freedom arrives. If kids see that Mommy's ride is late, they know they have extra time to harass Mommy and guilt her into staying home. There is nothing worse than sitting in a car with a woman whose kids have had an extra minute to play head games and make her feel like the mother from hell for abandoning them for a selfish evening out. It's this sense of guilt that can really deflate the mood of an evening!

Take note: it's important to decide ahead of time who will be the chauffeur. I know you're all thinking "designated driver - how responsible." Well, I'm not. We follow that no drinking- no driving rule, but that's not the reason for determining the driver. The reason to decide ahead of time is that you all want to go together. This way no one misses out on any part of the conversation or gossip. Gossip is an integral part of these adventures. And there's nothing more annoying than having to repeat the same gossip again and again to the people who have come in different cars at different times. Rent a minivan if no one has one (yeah, right!) and ride together!

3. Never wait for your ride inside your home. Never, ever break this rule! Make the break from your family as quickly as possible. Throw kisses, yell goodbye and run out the door as fast as your feet can carry you. My friends and I wait outside our front doors or out in our driveways be it rain, snow, sleet or hail. One of us waits in the middle of the road and flags down the car when it comes into view. This is not recommended for two reasons: First, unless you wear reflective clothing, you may live out the proverbial "deer in the headlights" nightmare. And secondly, you can wave down the wrong car and find yourself on a date with the Dominos delivery guy.

4. Pick a movie that contains three basic elements: love, fantasy and good looking men. I probably don't have to explain this one, but hey, I'll do it anyway. You're going out to get away from it all. You don't want Sly Stallone blowing up buildings and wrecking cars. You don't want too see death and destruction, and you don't want to see bloodshed. This is the plot you want to see: two people fall in love; they get ripped apart by some tragic circumstance; and then fate and passion bring them back together again. You want to leave the theater weeping with clumps of mascara rolling down your cheeks. Then you know you've had fun.

5. Pick a restaurant that has great appetizers, desserts and non-cute waitresses. Women don't care about entrees. After the movie, we want wine and goodies to nosh on. We don't want some young, single, 20ish waitress who doesn't understand the ritual and urgency of Ladies Night Out. We want to order fried stuff and gooey, chocolate delights without a 100-pound waif staring at us, thinking we're frazzled, nearly middle-aged, pity cases living our lives in complete states of denial.

Oh, there is an important sub-rule to this restaurant thing. Arrange your party at the table according to food likes and dislikes. Put all the dessert people at one end of the table, and all the appetizer people at the other end. In this way, everyone can share their favorite foods without reaching over the table and interfering with other people's chewing and conversations. It's just good etiquette.

Well, that's pretty much the secret to a good night out. There's nothing complicated to it. It just takes solid planning, meticulous time keeping, and a souped up minivan that can go from 0 to 60 as it pulls away from the curb.

The Laundry Game

One morning last week, I experienced what some people would call a revelation. This great awakening occurred as I was attempting to carry a pile of dirty clothes down the steps to the laundry room. Unbeknownst to me, my dog, was chasing her tennis ball down those same steps at the same time I was blindly making my journey. What ensued I do not know. All I can tell you is that somehow I wound up at the bottom of the stairs, sitting in a pile of dirty clothes screaming out curse words that I didn't know I knew.

It was during this string of verbal expletives that this intense feeling came over me. At first, I thought it was just the pain in my backside -- a consequence of tumbling down four steps. But then I realized it wasn't physical pain; it was emotional pain. And this pain said in a very loud voice that sounded remarkably like my own:

"I hate laundry! I hate everything about it! I hate sorting. I hate folding. I hate those damn clothes that have to go in the gentle cycle! I hate fabric softener! And most of all I hate static cling!"

It's funny, but once I got that out of my system, a sense of calm came over me. And this was good because I knew that no matter how many tumbles I would take down those steps in the future, the laundry task would still always belong to me.

Now, I hear some women out there saying, "Why don't you just get your husband to do the laundry?"

Well, I do. In all fairness to my husband, he does do laundry IF I ask him. This is an important IF. According to my friends, my husband is like most men. They don't take the initiative to do laundry. Now, don't get upset, men. It's not your fault. Men don't realize laundry has to be done because their closets and drawers are always crammed with clean clothes. Somehow, men accumulate a year-long supply of socks, underwear and shirts. Where do these clothes come from?

This is one of the greatest mysteries about laundry: it has multiplication properties. Laundry breeds. I have noticed that if I leave a pile of clothes on the laundry room floor for a day, the pile grows. Now, my husband says that's impossible. His argument is that the clothes were all bunched together in the hamper. And when I throw them on the floor they have more room to spread out and un-jumble themselves. But, if that's the case, how come I find clothes in the pile I do not recognize. I think dirty clothes spawn new clothes.

People for years have wondered how come there's always one sock that gets lost in the wash. I don't think a sock gets lost. I think that the unpaired sock is a new sock-- a baby sock that was created by that pile of living, dirty laundry.

You want more proof, here it is. We are three people in my house. My daughter wears a uniform to school every day. How is it then, that I have to do approximately nine loads of laundry a week. There's no possible way we are wearing all these clothes. My hamper is always filled -- so much so that my husband maintains he can't fit his dirty stuff in there. This is why he must drop his dirty clothes on the bedroom floor.

I know you're all thinking, "She's gone over that edge again. She probably hit her head at the bottom of those steps instead of her backside." But that's not so. I get frustrated with laundry because it's a never-ending battle. The moment the hamper empties, something dirty finds its way in it. And because of this, most women will describe laundry as a futile job. And, yes, it is still a woman's job. According to one government study, 92 percent of all laundry is done by women. And all the modern innovations to help women do laundry have only served to make us do more things to laundry. Now, instead of rinsing our clothes in the cold stream like the pioneer women use to do, we pre-sort, pre-soak, soften, and de-cling our garments. And when all else fails, and we can't clean our clothes properly, we schlep them into the car and bring them to someone else who can.

Doing laundry is a no-win proposition. There doesn't seem to be an answer -- unless the people who make Pampers could come up with fashionable disposable clothes. Now, that would be a time saver.

Money Can't Buy Love -- or Can It?

I don't know how to break this to my fellow members of the female sex, but science has proved that we women are shallow. According to a UCLA psychological study, women consider money a major factor when contemplating marriage. In fact, a mate's ability to make money is more important his physical appearance, his educational background, his occupation or his religious beliefs. Women want a profitable bottom line, and we're willing to overlook other flaws to get it. A man could be a homely, illiterate, gangster who belongs to some weird, radical cult. But if he's rich, we'll marry him.

Now, I can hear the men out there shaking their heads in disgust.

"Tsk, tsk," they're saying. "How can you women put so much emphasis on the almighty dollar?"

Well, Gentlemen, before you don those halos, let me enlighten you on what the study said about the male sex. Money is important to men too. Men still rank physical beauty as a higher priority than money when it comes to choosing a spouse, but money and potential earnings is closing in quickly. Essentially, men now want a woman to be rich and beautiful. Men want a woman who not only looks like Christie Brinkley, but one who will bring home the paycheck like Christie Brinkley. What does this say? It says that men are wading in the same shallow waters as women.

For the sake of argument, let's assume this study is accurate. As such, I am compelled to ask this question. What is wrong with us? Since when did our ability or lack of ability to live the "good life" mean the difference between a fling and a lifelong commitment? What happened to traits like sensitivity, compassion -- sanity? Have we abandoned these once-important qualities for a Gucci purse and a Lexus?

With money such a priority in today's world, how do people seek out potential mates? How do they let others know immediately that they are financially successful? One way would be to tape their income tax returns to their chests. This would eliminate a lot of mystery. Right off the bat, people could find out someone's name, occupation, gross income -- even real estate and investment holdings.

It's easy to see that this relationship study struck a big nerve with me. I always thought marriage was about two people who adored each other. Now this study makes it sound like marriage is nothing more than a prenuptial agreement with an occasional moment of passion thrown in.

Love should be like it is in romance novels: adventurous, monogamous, eternal and tax exempt. No one in those books throws in the towel because the love of their lives doesn't make a million bucks a year. And look at all the romantic movies. Men and women in love overcome horrible adversity to be together. Money is never a reason for romance. If anything, money is the obstacle which stands in the way of eternal bliss. In the movies, the heroes give up the money all for the sake of love.

I know the movies are only fantasy. But somewhere between that fantasy and reality lies true love.

Believe me, I'm not naive. I like having an employed spouse. I can say in all honesty, that I have never fantasized about being married to a homeless guy who lives in a cardboard box. I like having my charge accounts in good standing. But I would hope that if all the perks of financial stability were to disappear, my marriage would remain intact. If it didn't, there is no doubt that it's demise would be my fault. I know my husband married me because he liked me despite the fact I bore no resemblance to Christie Brinkley or any other model. I know he had to truly like me because there's no way he married me for economic security. No one marries a writer for that.

Overwhelmed Women's Week

I was driving back through a nearby town when I noticed a banner draped across the street hanging from two lamp posts. It read, "May 4 - May 10 -- National Drinking Water Week". I was intrigued. I never knew drinking water had a whole week completely devoted to it. It just never seemed to me to be a topic upon which the general population needed a whole week to reflect. But guess what? I Googled National Drinking Water Week, and I found out what the week was all about. It is a great educational week. It encourages people to learn how to take of our water supply.

But the whole week thing got me thinking. We dedicate weeks for every topic or cause under the sun. We used to have special designated days for all these causes but in today's hectic world, apparently single special days do not provide enough time to get in everything we need to accomplish. So, it was inevitable that someone would come up with the idea of full-week dedications.

With this in mind, I began to think about the possibility of having a week of my own. I know that sounds egotistical, so to assuage some of you out there who think I might be too self-important, I'm willing to make a compromise. We could make it "Overworked Women's Week." I know there is Mother's Day, but that is all it is -- one day. And there are plenty of women out there who aren't mothers but deserve a week of recognition as well.

The longer I mulled the idea over in my head, the more I thought that it could work. Since we women live such diverse lives, we could each design a week to fit our needs. While some women may prefer a paid vacation, others may prefer to make their own fantasy week. I began to think what my week might entail:

A Ticker Tape Parade through My House

Okay. This is not very practical, but who cares. It is my week. The parade doesn't have to be extravagant. I'll run on the treadmill while my husband and daughter throw roses at my feet (de-thorned, of course). They'll bow down as I run in place and they will say, "Thank you for doing everything you do. You are wonderful."

Each day of the special week, professionals will come to clean, do laundry, iron and cook.

I don't think I need to explain this fantasy activity. Just the thought of people taking care of everything in the house conjures up images of freedom, relaxation and peace of mind. Of course, this cleaning gift would be no fun if I couldn't brag about it to every other woman on the face of the earth. So, to bring this about, news bulletins announcing my week and its daily events will be broadcast all over the world. I think the president himself should host a special news conference personally dedicating my week to me.

A Banquet in My Honor

At this formal event, no one is allowed to appear more attractive than me. I get to pick the guest list, and they all have to come and sit where I put them. I do not care who is fighting with whom. People will come, be polite to each other, will not criticize each other and laugh all night. Those are the rules.

A Full-Hour Massage

For my final event of my special week, I am ordering a full-hour massage. I want the aromatherapy candles, mood music and a massage that will make my muscles feel as if they are 10-years-old again. Okay, I'll take muscles of a 20-year-old. Either way, I think this last bit of indulgence will be the crowning touch on a week whose effects will last me until next year's Overwhelmed Women's Week. I am already planning the festivities.

The Nagging Principle

I heard a report on the radio about a study which focused on nagging. According to the scientists who conducted the study, women nag more than men. You know, I'm not at all surprised by this. While I rarely nag my husband (and he will attest to this if he knows what's good for him), I do see how it goes on in other households. I also see the benefit of it. Even the scientists say women nag because we get results. They may be temporary results, but they are results nonetheless.

The scientists went on to report that men experience little benefit from nagging their wives. Women do not respond to men's nagging. It seems the male sex just doesn't know how to nag properly. Women, on the other hand, possess a natural inclination to nag. Apparently, we can now affirm that nagging is in our genetic makeup. Yes, the ability to nag is as natural to women as ovaries and cellulite.

While some men try to acquire this ability, they're usually unsuccessful mainly because scientists say they pick impossible topics to nag about: sex and money. These are two things in a household women ultimately control. If men are going to nag, they should pick topics that most women do not have time to care about such as putting the TV remote in a safe place or changing the oil in the car before the warning light on the dashboard has been on for two weeks. These are naggable subjects.

What do women nag about according to the study? Household chores headed the list. Personally, I can vouch for this finding. This is why I nag, and this is how I nag. I make sure not to nag on a daily basis. I do this for two reasons: first, I know if I nag too much, my husband will tune me out. He is extremely good at this. Secondly, I like to save up my nags so when I let loose it is a nagging explosion, and nothing gets results quicker. A nagging explosion is a scary thing to watch and nobody knows this better than my husband. I do have advice for women who want to try my method of nagging. Schedule your blowups on a regular basis. Avoid using the PMS excuse. Men are inundated with PMS talk. Men ignore women's complaints because they attribute everything to hormonal changes. Getting him to take nagging seriously is very important. I time my nagging to occur quarterly - at the same time I pay my estimated taxes. When I write out the check to the federal government, I plan my nagging routine.

Nagging does not need an element of surprise. In fact, for my husband, the anticipation that the nagging is on its way is far worse than the actual nagging. This also gives him the opportunity to shape up and avoid any confrontation. It puts some of the control back in his hands. If he chooses to ignore the warning signs and the impending explosion date, then he really has no one else to blame for the nagging explosion but himself. I think this is a fair system.

One last thing about nagging: Nagging does not change behavior permanently. Nagging is a band-aid and nothing more. It fixes things for a while, and then we slowly slip back into the same old behavior. Is this bad? Not really. Nagging gives husbands and wives something to talk about. Nagging brings back vital, passionate emotion, and it gives us a diversion from our everyday humdrum patterns of behavior. Nagging rids our bodies of stress and forces couples and families to work together to accomplish a common goal even if that common goal is nothing more than scrubbing the bathroom floor or cleaning out the attic.

Yes, at times, nagging is repulsive. Yet, at other times, nagging is the catalyst that makes a splintered marriage whole again. And if you men out there don't believe that-- well, tough. Women like nagging, and if those scientists are right, nagging is here to stay.

My Office Assistants

I am sitting here in my home office jotting down some thoughts and sneaking a peak at TV. There is no one here with me except my constant companions, Muffie and LuLu—my two pooches. They are so devoted to my work. They listen to me when I read things aloud, they bark when my fax goes off. In her younger days, Muffie would even rip the paper off of the fax machine and bring it to me. Now, she just growls at the noise.

My friend has two part-time assistants. She has had to teach them both the workings of the fax over and over. They don't care about her deadlines. They only care about their set hours. My dogs keep no set hours. They are by my side through stressful deadlines, the most horrendous moments of writer's block, and the pain of rejection letters. We use those bad letters to wipe their paws on rainy days. They even greet the mailman, UPS and FED EX guys for me. I love that they do that, but I'm not quite sure if the delivery men like it.

My dogs never criticize my work, and they never complain about overtime, a lack of a medical plan or the outside bathroom facilities. Muffie and LuLu are also great lunch companions. They eat whatever I eat, and I never have to treat them to restaurant food except on their birthdays when I take them through the drive-thru at Burger King.

Another major advantage of my office cronies is their lack of legal knowledge. They will never sue me for political incorrectness. I can host Christmas parties and have a tree without worrying that the ACLU will pay me a visit for not recognizing any other December holidays. Now, if any of my dogs expressed an interest in other holidays, I would gladly and wholeheartedly display other symbols, but I don't feel the pressure at this point.

I listen to the trials and tribulations of other writers who have human office assistants and I am grateful for my canine staff. I don't have to deal with office politics unless of course one pooch thinks the other is getting more treats or hugs. They never have to worry about dressing up for me, and I don't have to dress up for them. Every day is casual Friday. In fact, they go around nude – except for their bandanas, of course.

I'm hoping that my office assistants will stay with me forever. I offer a great office environment with outstanding benefits that consist of all the dog treats, hugs and cuddles they want plus regular vet visits and at least three romps in the backyard a day.
Sometimes, they even enjoy taking a mid-day power nap with me, and they have no expectations for promotions for doing so.

I like the dynamics of my office, and I would hate to ruin it by hiring humans. It's true we work in a solitary existence, but for my dogs and myself it is office living at its best. .

Self-Improvement for the New Year

At the end of each year, I come to the same conclusion: I need work. I'm not talking employment (although that would be nice); I'm talking body and mind rebuilding. I know I'm not the only one out there who feels this way. Millions of people make the annual commitment to restructure their lives so they can enjoy more fulfilling and satisfying existences.

To be honest, I don't mind making this commitment. I like the feeling that I'm about to embark on a physical and spiritual journey that will improve my life and coax me into becoming a better person. This year, I've come up with a short list of self-improvement goals that I think myself and my family can live with. Will my family be supportive of what I hope to accomplish? I don't know. My husband and daughter will need time to adjust to my goals and the reasons why I feel I need to reach those goals. At first, they'll fret the changes. They'll detest the inevitable crankiness that will accompany my pangs for renewal. They'll fight me, but once they realize that they can support me or leave town, they'll back me up me up completely.

Truthfully, few of my goals require any assistance from them. But it would be nice to know that if I find myself in a crunch, they will be there to lend a hand and comfort me -- without yelling at me. So, with no further ado, let me tell you what I hope to accomplish this year.

I want to balance my checkbook:

This isn't exactly accurate. I don't care if I balance it. I just want to have a ballpark figure of what's really in my checkbook. Direct deposit, online banking and the convenient world of ATM machines haves completely screwed me up. I have guessed about the amount in my checking account for the last three years. I hold my breath every time I use my ATM card in a store. I pray fervently that the machine will not reject my bid for money. My worst fear is that I'll be in line and a sarcastic cashier will say:

"I'm sorry, but the computer has said we can't process your transaction. Apparently, you're broke." I've seen this happen. I've witnessed the humiliation, and I know I can't take it. I would be stammering to the whole store, "I do have money – not a lot, but enough for this, I swear! I just transferred it to my checking account. It must have become caught up in some computer glitch."

And as we all know, no one ever believes anyone who claims this as their defense. What I need to do is find a way to reconcile what I think is in my checking account to what the bank thinks is in my checking account. Frankly, I trust me more these days now that we know how careless the banking industry has been in the last few years.

I'm going to lose 10 pounds:

I know everyone says they're going to lose weight, but not the way I'm going to lose weight. I'm going to find a super diet which allows me to eat whatever I want; a diet which frowns on exercise; a diet which extols the virtue of ice cream and fatty foods and a diet that still promises me a 10-pound weight reduction within two weeks. And by the way, not only will this diet drop unnecessary weight, but it will tone and lift my body in all the right places. Eliminated forever will be cellulite, and those Jell-O wiggles that seem to be developing under my upper arms. It is my objective to be firm, thin and able to wear slim fit jeans by Valentine's Day.

I'm Throwing Gossip Out of My Life:

I am adopting a new rule. There will be no snickering, no complaining, and no passing on of information on my part to any other soul. However, for the record, you should all know I cannot control what other people do. So, if I happen to be in earshot of any kind of gossip, I will try to stop it immediately as soon as I ascertain if this gossip is true or false. Hey, I can't scold people for gossiping if I I'm unsure if what they're saying is gossip or not! Once, I find out all the details, I'll nip all rumors right in the bud. See, I can become a better person.

I'm going to learn many lessons from these objectives. I purposely picked goals that I can accomplish in due time. I thought about including a revenge goal on people who did me wrong this year. I do not have a formal list, but you know who you are. I won't waste my time on vengeance. Karma will get you in its own good time. Instead, I'm going to learn commitment, determination and the inevitable truth that next year I'll probably be shooting for the same goals again. Sorry to say, but restructuring the mind and body takes more than a one-year plan. It takes a daily practice schedule.

Poop Comes in all Forms

I was at the dry cleaners the other day dropping off my husband's dress shirts. As I waited in line, a man came in and asked if he could put his business card on this community bulletin board that was in the front of the shop.

His business caught my eye as he was a new franchisee for a company whose service includes picking up your dog's poop in your backyard on a weekly basis. For as little as $30 per week, you never have to take out that old shovel or pooper scooper again. My first reaction was that once a week would never work for me. I have two dogs who are prolific poopers. If I waited for an entire week, I could not even tip toe through my yard without stepping in something.

Stupidly, I did strike up a conversation with this intrepid entrepreneur. "Gee, I should put my business card up there. You never know who might read this bulletin board."

To which he said, "What do you do?"

To which I said, "I have a positive mindset website. I write daily words of encouragement and poetry." I tried to make the description brief as I saw his eyes rolling back into his head.

Then he said. "It's amazing how easily crap sells!"

I admit that at first I thought it was a joke because here he was picking up crap for a living, and I thought he was poking fun at me as some miserable people do because they believe that positive thinking is a load of crap, and they don't get that this is why they lead miserable lives. However, this man had not made the same connection as I did.

These thoughts ran through my brain, but not out of my mouth. I counted to 10 and took a deep breath and said in a calm voice, "You pick up dog poop for a living, and you think what I do is crap?"

He just glared at me and said "I don't sell crap, I remove it."

I wanted to say something truly mean back, but I decided to be the better person. Instead, I told him in an ever so gentle tone to take my card, and maybe, I could help him develop a better attitude on life. I also told him that his present attitude is perfect for what he chose to do for a living as you reap what you sow.

He still didn't get it. He stuffed the card in his pocket and walked out thinking that he was somehow above me. I guess practically speaking, it is important to have a clear yard, but to me, it is still more important to have a clear mind. I guess in truth, we both try to get rid of the poop that can damage our lives.

2012 Beam Me Up I am Ready

A few weeks ago, I was a guest a dinner party that was supposed to be celebrating a "50th" birthday of a friend of mine. The dinner was wonderful, and for the most part, the company was animated and refreshing. Everyone was relaxed and having a good time, until one of the guests decided to take on the role of "party annihilator".

I don't even know how it started, but I think someone made a joke about the economy. Well, this one joke caused this one guy to go into this freaky rant about the upcoming end of the world, which as we all know (unless you don't have a TV in your home), is coming on December 21, 2012.

Let me just say this, if 2012 is the end of the world and so many people believe this to be, why is anyone still worried about the financial crisis? Hell, if it is the end of the world, everyone go out and charge up a storm because no one is going to be around to give a hoot if you pay anything back or if you have an 800 or 300 credit score.

Personally, if December 21, 2012 is the end, I plan on going out on my front porch and breathing deeply. I do not have that "let me re-create the world survivor instinct". Truthfully, I probably don't have the ovaries to re-populate the world anymore, so my stock value in the whole rebuilding the planet scenario is minimal at best. I also do not possess the survivor skills that one might need in this doomsday environment. I am not even a good camper. I failed that badge in the Girl Scouts. I cannot imagine how bad I would be at digging through obliterated cities looking for morsels of food and clean water. I am not a pampered princess, but I do need some basic necessities to live: food, water, soft toilet paper, an internet connection and caffeine.

If these necessities are not going to be available, I might as well run into the explosion or tornado or earthquake or whatever is coming and kiss this life goodbye. I am hoping that God is as merciful as I have been taught and He says, "Come on in, you've made it to heaven!" If that is the case, then beam me up because heaven has got to be a lot better than chewing open cans of beans or cat food and dining on this fare after the disaster.

I have a very naïve theory on 2012. I think that the Mayan priests and scholars just stopped keeping track. Maybe they got bored of working out the calendars for so many centuries ahead. Maybe, they decided to take a coffee break or vacation and never went back to finishing them, or maybe one priest said to the other.

"We went through most of 2012. That's enough. Who is even going to remember us by then? I am sure they will have a more sophisticated method of timekeeping by the time that date rolls around. They can finish the calendar themselves. Let's go get a drink instead."

Who knows what will be? The thing is we waste so much time worrying about stuff that might never become a factor in our lives. Our job on this planet, now, is to take care of each other and make our present lives better so that our children's lives will be better and so on. Maybe the end of the world is around the corner or maybe there isn't an end.

We cannot control what happens in 2012 or tomorrow. We are guaranteed today, so find your joy, live your life, love your neighbor and pray. The rest is out of our hands.

The Dog and the Remote

After finishing a phone interview for an article I was writing, I decided to take a lunch break and watch a scary movie on the TV in my family room. Usually, I do not put on the TV until all my work was done, but it was Halloween and there were all my favorite scary flicks on, so I broke my rule.

I flicked on the TV with the remote and went upstairs to get a cup of coffee. When I came down, one of my dogs, my black lab/shepherd/ moose mix, had made herself at home on the sofa. Under her paw was the remote.

As I got closer to the TV, I realized that my mutt had accidentally pressed a button with her paw. I knew this because there was a notice on the screen telling me to confirm the order for a pay-for-view special on some kind of wrestling or fighting thing that came with a $29.95 price tag.

My first reaction was to dart toward the sofa and grab the remote. However, the pup was in play mode. She saw my face, and I guess she thought it was frolic time. She raised up her floppy ears and sat up straight; her paw still sat dangerously close to the remote. I had one chance to make a move and cancel that pricey cable feature.

I put down my coffee and nonchalantly walked my way over to the sofa trying not to draw attention to the fact that I was circling around her ready to attack. I could feel my dog's eyes follow me across the room. It was if she knew what I was thinking. Her paw moved the remote closer to her body. As I approached, I saw my dog's tail wag with glee. She wore a silly smile that seemed to say; "I may be the dog, but I am the one really in command."

This was not going to be easy. She wanted to pounce and play, and I wanted the remote. I made a quick dash and dove to the sofa. I swear that I saw it all happening in slow motion. As my body flew to the couch, she lifted up her paw(and I think intentionally) banged it down on the remote. In one quick instant, she confirmed the $29.95 pay-per-view. When I hit the sofa, she licked the top of my head as if to say, "Sorry, no hard feelings?"

I tried to call my cable operator and explain the situation, but dogs playing with the remote are not a legitimate excuse, so we will watch this wrestling thing. Who knows, maybe it really was something she wanted to see. I guess if she can handle the remote, she can pick out shows too.

What Happened To My Pot Holders?

I was in my bedroom when I heard the familiar blast of the kitchen smoke alarm. I knew it could only mean one thing: dinner was ready. So, I scurried downstairs and opened the oven door to confirm my theory. I knew from the looks of that dinner that time was of the essence. So, I quickly opened the drawer next to the stove and reached in to retrieve my potholders.

But there were no potholders. There were no oven mitts. There wasn't even a dish towel. I frantically searched the drawer. I scooped out matches, birthday candles, rubber bands, toothpicks, Wash and Dry towelettes, hot glue sticks and old coupons. But no pot holders.

"Where are they?" I asked nervously as I watched my meat turn darker before my eyes. "They must be in this kitchen somewhere."

So, I emptied out two other drawers. And still no pot holders. Finally, I ran upstairs to the bathroom linen closet. I pulled two wash cloths off the shelf and used them to rescue my overdone dinner.

While it's true that everything worked out okay, the mystery remains: What happened to the potholders? Why were they not in the potholder drawer? The answer is simple. I don't have a potholder drawer anymore. Apparently, junk has taken over that drawer. And that's not the only drawer where this has happened.

I am blessed with a big kitchen which is lined with cabinets, drawers and shelves. The people who owned the house before us must have liked cupboards because they put in a lot of them. It amazes me that a house which has only three people and two dogs living in it, can have every cupboard and drawer filled with junk. How could we have so much junk?

I've got stuff in those drawers and cupboards I can't identify. There are photos from my engagement party in the good silver drawer. How did they get there?

In another kitchen drawer, I found every instruction manual to every appliance we have owned. Inside these manuals, I found the filled-out warranty cards which I probably should have mailed in when we bought most of those appliances many years ago. I'm just guessing, but I think the warranties are pretty useless now.

In truth, I clean out these drawers every few years. It takes two lawn-sized, plastic bags to get rid of the unnecessary clutter. I throw out chewed pencils, dried-out markers, burnt candles, old school correspondence and my favorite, de-magnetized refrigerator magnets. But the junk always reappears. It's like the drawers possess a mind of their own. They seem to have the power to conceal the junk. They let me think I got rid of it, but it is just an illusion.

My husband and daughter think I worry too much about the drawers.

"So, they're filled with stuff, so what. That's their job to hold our stuff," my husband says in his logically when I start to rant over the clutter which has accumulated. "They're good at their job. We know where all our things are. We just have to dig for them a little."

But guess what? He is not so laid back about the drawer mess when he's trying to find something. When this happens, the world must come to a complete stop until we locate what he needs.

"Where's the good barbecue brush? I can't find a thing in these drawers! I can't cook without my good brush. Help me out! Everyone search!"

We leave no drawer untouched. By the time we find what he's looking for, the kitchen looks as if a nuclear bomb landed in the middle of it. When it's over, I stand there shell shocked, surveying the damage and I swear,

"As God as my witness, I will clear this junk out. If it takes me the rest of my life, I will triumph over it."

Procrastination, Thy Name is Husband

In our house, my husband has two assigned responsibilities: trash and taxes. There are other chores we split between us, but these are his priority tasks during the year. While I admit these two responsibilities require some attention to detail, I do not think they are beyond the mental capabilities of a man who holds both college and post-graduate degrees. Granted, trash is more complicated these days. No longer is it just a hefty bag out on the curb. There is a certain amount of sorting and stacking required now that recycling plays such a dominant role in garbage removal. But even with all these changes, I still don't see how taking out the trash can pose so much difficulty. I think it's pretty simple to remember: The trash men come on Tuesdays for all types of garbage and on Fridays for unrecyclable garbage.

But apparently, I'm wrong. it's not that simple. For why else do I crawl out of bed at the crack of dawn on Tuesdays to drag that stupid recycling bin out to the curb? Is it because I want to scare the poor trash men with my appearance at that early hour? No, that is just an added bonus. Is it because I enjoy showing the entire neighborhood my colorful collection of flannel sleepwear and wooly socks? No, I don't think that is the reason either. The reason I am outside on my curb at dawn is because my husband never puts out the bin the night before trash pick-up despite my constant nagging to accomplish this simple feat.

"I'll do it later on," he always says as he ignores me and clicks the remote, or "I'll do it before I go to work in the morning."

Uh-huh. I put these words in the same category with "The check is in the mail," and "I'll respect you in the morning."

I complain about the trash situation in my house because I am at a loss to understand why he wants so desperately to hold onto it. I plead with him,

"Why can't the nice trash men take our garbage? They want it; we don't. Let them have it!"

He, of course, has no answer for me, so we remain at a standstill on this issue. Taxes, his other duty, present a different obstacle for us. I admit I understand his hesitation about doing our taxes. It's very difficult to part with money. He's not good at it. (Luckily, I'm good enough at it for both of us.) But I do see the pain in his face when he's preparing the various forms, and this does hurt me deeply. What complicates our tax situation is the filling out of my Schedule C. Usually, this process results in at least one heated argument about my lack of organizational skills where I become grossly offended by his remarks and stomp off in a major huff. He then spends the remaining days of the week trying to make up for his callous comments which he probably had every right to make, but was dumb enough to verbalize.

This year, I thought we avoided this marital strife. I insisted we do our federal returns in February. This worked out great. Everything was off to the government without any pressure, and it was the first tax season that a feeling of calm hovered over our home -- until I started to nag him about state and local taxes.

"When are we going to do those?" I would ask at least once a week.

"We'll get them done. They're just a couple of forms. We have time."

Guess where we spent the morning of April 15th? At the post office mailing out forms with the other procrastinators.

By midmorning of the 15th, it was easy to see that I was not happy with his procrastination.

"You're a good sport," he told me lovingly. "I promise next year will be different. We'll do everything early, so these taxes won't be hanging over our heads."

I think he must have sensed that I was just a tad ticked off at him. For later that afternoon, I looked out the window and noticed that the recycling bin and the large trash container were already out by the curb waiting for the next day's pick-up.

A Crown for My Own

Anyone who has raised a daughter has come into contact with tiaras – yes those little crowns that allow girls to take on the personas of princesses for dance recitals, proms, birthdays and weddings. The funny thing about tiaras is that they really do make someone feel special. As soon as a girl of any age puts on one of these crowns, her shoulders go back and a glow comes over her. It does not matter if the tiara is made of plastic, rhinestone or diamonds. They still shine and make the girls shine with them.

Being a tee shirt and jeans type of person, tiaras never really appealed to me, but I have to say that one time as I watched a tiara sparkle on my daughter's head during a dance recital, I thought how nice it would be to have my own crown. I mentioned this to my husband, who quickly asked,

"What would you do with one if you owned it?" she asked.

"I would just wear it -- all the time. It would be my way of showing people that I am the queen, and they better not mess with me."

Of course, at that moment I was kidding. But the more I thought about it, the more I liked the idea of wearing a crown whenever the mood hit me. Let's face it, tiaras can come with benefits.

First of all, just because they sparkle, tiaras get attention. Think about it. You're trying to find someone to help you in a store. The clerks could usually care less whether they assist you or not. But wear a tiara into the store, and watch the help gravitate to you. Store employees would probably fall all over themselves to wait on royalty. Just look what wearing a crown does for Queen Elizabeth or Miss America. The everyday person responds to jeweled headgear. They see anyone wearing that kind of accessory as important.

Of course, there is the possibility that wearing a crown, especially a costume crown, could get you labeled as an unstable individual. Frankly, that label never bothered me much. And if you can live with some ridicule, go out and buy yourself the best, darn crown you can find.

This brings me to reason number two for wearing a tiara: intimidation

Picture this scenario. Your family is taking advantage of you again. You've run your thousandth errand; you've cooked, cleaned and carpooled. Now, all you want is a dinner out or possession of the TV remote control. Your family scoffs at your wishes. What do you do? Do you sulk or scream about how you're treated like a slave? No. You put on a crown and threaten to walk out the front door and go to the grocery store. I guarantee within seconds, you will have dinner delivered to you in bed and the remote control sitting on your lap.

You see, a tiara might make you feel special, but the reality is it will do nothing to boost your family's image in the community. So, the next time your family takes advantage of your good nature, whip out your crown and say calmly,

"Get this straight. I am the royal, head honcho of this abode, and tonight, you people are my serfs and court jesters. Either you obey my rule, or my crown and I are cruising the neighborhood."

Okay, so I admit that I don't have the guts to do the crown thing -- not in public anyway, and unfortunately, my husband knows that. But I still think it would be a grand idea to own a crown and wear it around the house when you get depressed or frustrated with life. I would think that wearing even a fake crown has got to boost one's spirits. The more I think about it, I have some of my daughter's old tiaras in a box in the attic. I'm going to claim one of them, and put it on anytime I think the blues may hit. After all, there's nothing wrong with feeling like "Queen for a Day."

Amusement Park Rides Are No Ticket to Fun for Me

As another summer approaches, I know what lies ahead. There will be trips to the beach, days at the pool, and of course, those family outings to my favorite place: the amusement park. For the record, I must say that amusement parks hold very little amusement for me. Don't get me wrong. I like spending the day with my husband and daughter. I like scouring the gift shops for funny hats, refrigerator magnets and coffee mugs that bear the name of whatever theme park we visit. I enjoy the dolphin shows, animal safaris and the musical extravaganzas these parks produce. I don't even mind the $6.50 cheeseburgers. But I have to admit, that I would like these parks a whole lot better if they didn't have rides. Yes, it is true: I am a ride weenie.

I'm not exactly sure when I became a ride weenie. I think I was born that way. I never remember looking up at a roller coaster and saying, "Wow, that looks so scary. Please, Mommy let me go on it!"

No, I was the kid who prayed that I didn't meet the height requirements for rides or as the amusement park people call them -- attractions -- one term I will never understand. Anyway, I remember one time, hanging on to my mother's skirts pleading with her to take me off a ride.

"Please, I'll do anything you ask, just please, please don't make me do this." And my mother, seeing how desperate I was, took pity on me and gently pulled me off the wooden horse of the carousel. The next year, during my senior high school trip to the same park, I was much better.

Okay, maybe that is a bit of an exaggeration, but the basic truth is that even as I grew up, I never developed a desire to go on these death defying rides. I never saw the purpose of them. I don't think any of them offer amusement. I think they offer torture. And I have a problem with paying a lot of money for torture. In fact, I'm a person who believes torture should be free.

Unfortunately, my husband and daughter live for these rides. The faster they go; the happier they are. They want to experience the thrill of living on the edge. I don't need the edge. I like the middle ground -- it's safer. I guess what it comes down to is this: I need to see the logic behind these rides. If someone can explain to me what is so fun about plunging down five-story hills at 90 miles per hour, I'll rethink my fears. Is it the thrill of defying gravity that lures people to these frightening adventures? Is it because that for a few, brief moments, as you plummet down these man-made mountains, you enjoy losing function of your vital internal organs? As exciting as heart and kidney failure sound, it is not enough to inspire me to strap myself into some dinky little car to take part in a stare down with death.

You see, I really am a ride weenie. I must confess, I've turned other people into ride weenies too. In college, I went with some friends to an amusement park. I vowed to myself that on this one day, I would go on all the "terror" rides, and I did -- but mainly by myself. It seems that as I waited in line with my friends, I scared them out of their desire to experience the thrill of these rides. To this day, I don't know what I said that was so wrong. All I did was point out some minor concerns I had -- and still have. For example, why do high school kids who are not yet mature enough to operate cars, mature enough to operate the controls of the most horrific rides -- the ones which hurl people upside down at warp speeds? Also, why do all these attractions have those health warning signs posted at the front of their lines? You know those warnings. They suggest that anyone with any kind of respiratory, muscular, digestive, circulatory, neurological or reproductive condition, i.e. pregnancy, stay off the ride. In my estimation that's about 92 percent of the general population. And it amazes me that most people ignore the warnings and go on the rides anyway.

Now me, I heed those warnings. I think if the park people go to the trouble and expense of posting them on big, wooden signs at each individual ride, they must be serious, or more likely, well acquainted with the 16-year-olds who are operating those rides.

Okay, maybe I worry too much about the amusement park scene. Maybe, I should just let go and join my family in the thrill of living on the edge. Then again, maybe this year, I'll let them go by themselves. They can go off on their own and defy death. I'll use this time to take up a more stable hobby. How does bungi jumping sound?

The Romance Quotient

During a recent chat session with friends, our conversation naturally turned to the subject of marriage and romance. For the male gender, this is a no-win topic. Very few man fare well in this area. It's a mystery to me why this is so. Maybe we women expect too much. Maybe men don't understand what our concept of romance is all about. It is possible that the two sexes possess different definitions for romance. Well, if that's the case, here's a short test I've devised for all you guys. Five simple questions which will allow you to compare your idea of romance against the typical female standards. Please circle all answers that apply to your situation. Good Luck and may Cupid go with you!

1. The last time I brought flowers home to my wife:

A. Her birthday

B. Our anniversary

C. The last time I stayed out past 3 AM with my friends without calling home.

D. Hey, I gave her the extra carnations that were left over from her great aunt's funeral. They're flowers.

E. Never. I've never brought home flowers. They die within a day, and it is thirty bucks down the drain.

2. What was the last piece of jewelry you gave your wife?

A. An anniversary ring with a half-carat of diamonds embedded on a platinum band.

B. An anniversary ring with a small setting of diamonds and rubies around an 18 carat band.

C. An anniversary ring with cubic zirconias around a silver-plated band.

D. An anniversary ring with plastic, fake diamonds glued to an adjustable band.

E. I don't give jewelry because it's a lousy investment and has no practical purpose.

3. The last time I gave my wife chocolates:

A. Last Valentine's Day

B. Her Birthday

C. Our anniversary. I forgot about it, and the florist was closed. But luckily, the drug store was open, and they had these neat boxed candies on display for half off because it was two weeks after Valentine's Day.

D. The last time I stayed out until 3 AM with my friends without calling home.

E. The first time she had the courage to go to a Weight Watchers meeting.

4. Your wife feels fat and unattractive. To boost her spirits you:

A. Keep telling her she's just as beautiful as the day you married her.

B. Tell her that those 15 or 20 pounds she has packed on don't matter to you at all.

C. Assure her that all women who have gone through childbirth have those same pockets of fat on their thighs as well.

D. Buy for her the Cindy Crawford video workout collection so she, too, can get her body to look that perfect.

5. You and your wife have a spat in which she claims you are never there when she needs you. To make up with her you:

A. Apologize, tell her you were wrong and offer to do all the household chores for a month.

B. Apologize, tell her you were wrong and offer to take her out for a romantic dinner.

C. Apologize, tell her she deserves a rest and then go play a double round of golf.

D. Don't apologize and pretend that the whole fight never took place.

The test is over. Now, that you've completed it, let's review your answers. The scoring is very simple. If you had to read beyond answers A or B, you failed, and you're in a whole lot of trouble. But, there still may be hope as long as you want to make some changes. It may be a good idea to buy a self-help book on how to rekindle your relationship. You can take your spouse to one of those marriage seminars or go away for a weekend -- together would be best. Stop thinking about a trip to the grocery store as a night out. When your wife starts to travel down memory lane recalling the romantic moments of your lives together, enjoy it with her. Don't mar important memories of your marriage with comments like

"Oh, yeah, I remember that. That's the year the Giants won the Super Bowl for the first time."

Speaking as a woman, I say this: The slightest improvement in your attitude is so beneficial to the health of a marriage. And if this is not incentive, then perhaps this is: Remember there is no creature anywhere on this planet as dangerous as a woman who feels neglected or taken for granted.

And that, dear men, is advice you can take to the bank.

Telemarketers Bring Out the Worst in Me

I, like many Americans, hate telemarketers. I don't dislike them. I don't find them annoying. I hate them. Even though I am on no-call lists, some still get through, and they get through at the most inconvenient times. Telemarketers bug me because they invade my home by relying on two brutal sales approaches: insult and guilt.

One afternoon, I picked up the telephone and was greeted by a female voice blurting out,

"Can I speak to Edward Cavana?"

She mistakenly rhymed the name with banana.

"No, I'm sorry, and the name is pronounced. Cav-an-aw," I corrected her. "It ends in AW, and no he's not here."

"Okay. Is Edward home?" She asked again. I was stunned. I thought it must be a de ja vu thing. No one could be this dense. But, she wasn't listening. She didn't care what my answer was. She droned on in a monotonous voice demanding to know when he would be in so she could talk with him. She was stuck on this point which could only mean one thing: she was reading from a script in front of her. That's the charm of telemarketers. They say only what the script tells them to say. They can't digress from their script. If they do, they lose their train of thought and have to start all over again.

It's no secret that this telemarketer had me annoyed, but I did do my best to respond to her request politely.

"No, Edward is not here, but this is his wife. May I help you?"

"No, what time will he be home, Mrs. Ca-van- a?" again with the same question and the same mispronunciation. "I need to speak to him about your family's financial investments."

"You do, do you? Well, you can talk to me, Mrs. Ca-va-na. (I mispronounced it just to irk her and show her I was not to be intimidated.) I'm part of the family, you know."

I heard her sigh with frustration. "I'd prefer to talk with Mr. CAV-AN- AW directly," she corrected herself. "Since you're home, he's probably at work and, therefore, the person in charge of the finances."

I couldn't figure out if this woman was in some kind of a snit or just naturally rude. Either way, this was not her day. She was about to have a head on collision with me, and she had no clue what she was in for.

I blasted her. I preached to her about the lack of respect she conveyed to me -- another woman. I chastised her for presuming I don't know anything about our investments or financial status. I threatened to sue her company with discrimination. I insisted on speaking to her supervisor. He got on the phone, and then I blasted him. I was in command!

When I hung up that phone, I was shaking with the thrill of victory. You know what is sad about this situation? It is not rare. My friends and I laugh at the abundance of phone calls we receive from people who still only want to speak to the man of the house. They call to pitch anything from carpet cleaning services to high-priced, replacement windows. I have only one question: who are these marketing gurus who believe that the men of America have this much financial power in their households? Boy, are they out of touch! Most men in America do not know where the checkbook is let alone how much is in it.

Let's move on to the second telemarketing tactic -- guilt. This is most effectively used by charities and non-profit organizations. A good, charity telemarketer can immediately immerse you, the potential gift giver, into a gut-wrenching story about a child in some horrible predicament who needs you, personally, to save his life. Well, for a while, I was on every charity's hit list. They probably had posters of me hanging in their offices with captions that read,

"Make everyone the sucker she is!"

I gave money to everyone -- the poor, the hungry, the ill, public television -- I was a sap! My husband would groan in disbelief every time one of these telemarketers snared me in a conversation. He would yell to me from across the room,

"Tell them 'NO!' and hang up."

I couldn't do it. I was trapped. Then I looked at my checkbook and realized that these contributions were depleting my funds for the essentials of living-- namely food and shelter.

I honestly tinkered with the idea of calling back some of these organizations which had received my generosity so willingly and demand they telemarket for me -- for now I was the poor, the hungry and the deprived! I didn't have the guts to do that, so I went another route. I learned to lie.

Now, when the telemarketers call me with some tear-my-heart-out, sob story, I beat them to the punch and deliver one of my own.

"No, I can't give to your cause today, because I need the money for my heart transplant next week" or "Gee, I'm sorry, but I'm saving up to send my sister's 11 children in Appalachia to the dentist for gum work."

No, it's not pretty and it's not nice, but dealing with charity is neither for the faint hearted nor the good natured. It's a war out there -- a war over emotions. And just so no one thinks I'm a horrible human being, I would like to say I do a great deal of volunteer work, and I still give money to worthy causes, but not through telemarketers . If I want to experience that enormous sense of guilt, I'll call my mother. Why should I give the privilege of bestowing such guilt upon me to a complete stranger when I know the woman who gave birth to me after hours and hours of labor will get such a thrill out of it?

A Shoulder to Cry On

We were driving back from my parents' house. We were on the New Jersey Turnpike and moving along somewhat slowly. We had just completed the tricky merge around Exit 8, and about 10,000 cars had not yet adjusted to the fact that the five lanes of highway were now three. We crawled along for a few minutes, biding our time with the rest of the cars. And then we stopped dead. But despite the delay, we were all polite and respectful of each other's space.

Suddenly, it happened. Somewhere from behind us a Cadillac zoomed by us at 80 m.p.h. He left us and all the other vehicles in the dust, laughing as he raced on. We all knew -- all of us on the road -- that we were victims of a shoulder maverick.

As the maverick passed by each car, you could see the drivers' and passengers' response to his actions. They made gestures at him in disgust. After my husband and I made our own separate remarks, (his were more colorful -- I was surprised!) I started to think about these people, these flagrant abusers of the road system. Who are they? Are there supernatural beings or traffic angels out there who handpick these daredevils to be shoulder riding mavericks? Do these supernatural forces say to them "Hey, you're better than everyone else, and your time is certainly more valuable? Ride that shoulder. Own that shoulder. Be that shoulder?"

Whether it's a supernatural thing or not, these people certainly think they are special because off they go without a care about anyone else on the road. For the mavericks, riding the shoulder is a thrill. They live for the adventure of not being spotted by the police. They thrive on their belief that everyone else on the road is envious of their spunk, their courage, and their complete disregard for road safety. What they don't realize is that everyone else on the road thinks of them as egotistical morons and hopes that the cops not only spot them, but ticket them, arrest them and possibly find some legal reason to shoot them. Unfortunately, that only happens in fairy tales.

While law abiding motorists may not be able to stop the shoulder mavericks, we can impede their progress by stopping their groupies better known as the shoulder maverick wannabes. You know these drivers. We have all seen them. These are the people who don't have the guts to go on the shoulder by themselves. They sit and fantasize about making that daring move, but they never go. They get fidgety and nervous, but they never turn that wheel and make a break for it until they see the shoulder maverick do it first. Then they hang out for a minute, making sure no police cruisers are around. When the coast is clear, they pull out onto the shoulder and follow their hero down the highway.

You would think that with all this practice driving down highways, some of these shoulder people would have learned how to drive well somewhere along the line. Let me illustrate my point with a typical encounter between normal drivers and the shoulder drivers during a rush hour traffic jam.

The maverick makes his move and coolly heads down the crowded highway speeding along the shoulder. Soon, the temptation to follow spurs the groupies into the shoulder lane as well. Then because there are too many groupies, the traffic builds on the shoulder causing a slow down on the shoulder comparable to that of the original traffic jam they worked so hard to avoid. Finally, down the road, the shoulder maverick and the followers make their first attempt to get back into the right lane and rejoin the rest of traffic. Well, by now, the law abiding motorists want nothing to do with the maverick or the groupies, so they cut these drivers off and refuse to let their vehicles into the lane. (Tractor trailer drivers are especially good at this tactic.) This causes a further slow down and creates a gridlock of merging traffic which makes the shoulder unavailable for any other driver who runs into legitimate car problems.

And what are the odds on the New Jersey Turnpike that a car will break down at this time? My best guess would be better than even money. So, a car goes kaput (usually in the left lane) forcing all the traffic to merge right. How can this be when the shoulder riders are merging left? Now, there is no room for anyone to merge anywhere, and the entire roadway becomes a parking lot and the leading item on the hourly traffic report.

Well, after much objective evaluation on the subject (the many times that I have been cut off and almost hit by shoulder mavericks and their groupies have not influenced my thinking whatsoever), I have come to the conclusion that riding the shoulder illegally should be a capital offense. Now, before everyone gets all riled up, let me say that I am not a person who normally favors capital punishment. But we really don't have to execute anyone. We can just scare them and tell them they may be executed for riding in the shoulder in the middle of a major traffic jam. Then when it comes time for sentencing, the judge can order them to do community service instead.

"Well, this is a capital offense," the judge could bellow in an authoritative tone, "but being it's your first offense, you can clean up the highway in one of those attractive, orange jumpsuits. But be warned! Next time, I'll send you to the chair!"

And the shoulder rider will cower with gratitude and say,

"Never again, Your Honor. I'll only ride in the correct, designated lanes. I give you my solemn vow."

Okay, the threat of death may be going too far. If we have to be nice and forgiving, I guess for most lane offenders, the embarrassment of being seen in public in those orange jumpsuits would be enough to keep them off the shoulders for many a year. I myself know that if a friend of mine was sentenced to pick up trash on the highway in one of those outfits, I'd be on the scene bright and early with camera in hand. I think a nice 8"x 10" picture to the offender's mother plus wallets distributed to approximately 50 of our closest and dearest friends should turn our special little shoulder maverick into a 50 m.p.h. right lane driver forever.

Day Of the Squirrel

A few years back, I returned home from the grocery store and was surprised that my 80-pound German Shepherd, Miss Muffie, did not greet me at the door in her usual, frantic fashion. After a few seconds, I called out to her. But she did not come. Growls and scratching sounds emanated from the kitchen. Cautiously, I made my way back, and there, I saw it -- a big, brown, fuzzy squirrel jumping up and down in a state of panic on the sill of my new, garden window, and the dog was standing at the sink in front of the window blocking the rodent's path to escape.

"Okay, "I told myself in a calm voice. "It's just a squirrel-- only a possibly rabid rodent, which by the way looks like it weighs 40 pounds. But you can handle this." But you know what? I couldn't handle it. I did not know how to handle squirrels. I had to kill a few roaches in my college dorm in New York City years ago, and I still have nightmares about it. For a squirrel, I would need therapy.

I ran quickly outside to the patio and grabbed a rake -- I don't have a clue why. I just knew I wanted it. I then propped open the patio door and banged on its window to direct the squirrel toward the way out, but it wouldn't budge. Miss Muffie was now starting to lunge at the creature. I didn't want her to kill the squirrel. I'm ashamed to admit it, but it wasn't because of any animal protection issue. I didn't want the rodent's blood in my kitchen or worse on my oriental rug in my living room! I ran and opened the front door as well hoping the squirrel would see that as a route to freedom.

This was obviously a very stupid squirrel. It didn't go anywhere near any of the doors. It scampered off through my dining room, into my living room knocking everything over in its path. Of course, my dog followed in hot pursuit, and I, with my rake in hand, chased the dog. We ran up the stairs; we ran down the stairs. Finally, the furry monster ran into our spare bedroom -- more commonly known as the Barbie room. I grabbed the dog before she ran into the room, and I pulled her out briskly. The squirrel crouched in the corner and shook with fear. Personally, I think it was overwhelmed by the hot pink paint, the Barbie border and the 1000 or so naked dolls strewn around the room. If I was that small, I know this room would frighten the hell out of me. Amazingly, I came to my senses and slammed the door shut trapping the rodent inside. Then I made plans.

I called my husband at work to calmly tell him of the situation. I thought I was doing pretty well. His voice mail came on and what I planned to say was,

"We have a squirrel in the house, what do you think is the correct procedure?" What came out was,

"Where are you? Why aren't you ever at your damn desk? Get home! There's a huge rodent in the Barbie room and it's chewing the heads off all the dolls!"

With that done, I hung up. I then tried his cell number. Voicemail again. So, I left another well thought out message. In the meantime, I called exterminator after exterminator. Very few handle squirrels. Finally, one nice guy answered the phone, and I said,

"Help me. I have a squirrel trapped in my bedroom, please come now."

The man must have sensed the panic in my voice. He took my address and told me he'd be there as soon as possible -- in about an hour and a half.

I don't think I need to mention that it was a long ninety minutes. While I waited, my husband called. He was very nice and supportive, but he didn't think there was any point to him making the half-hour trip home. He assured me he would keep in touch to make sure I was okay. When the exterminator did arrive, I met him at the door-- still carrying my rake, of course. We crept up into the hallway and prepared to fling open the door. We assumed "Starsky and Hutch" positions. I thought we should call for back up, but he assured me he could handle the perpetrator himself. He went in and shut the door behind him. I heard furniture move, and I thought,

"My God, the rabid rodent is eating him."

But within a minute he came out and announced, he didn't find the squirrel, and he thought I imagined it. He showed me a stuffed animal and said,

"This is probably what you saw."

"I don't think so," I chuckled politely while tightening the grip on my rake. "Come see the damage to my three-week old, garden, bay window which I assure you is not covered by homeowners insurance!"

He looked. He apologized. And then he went back into the room, and there he found the squirrel. I heard the window open, and the exterminator called,

"He's gone. He went out the window."

Then the nice man handed me a bill for $175. One hundred and seventy-five dollars for opening a window! I'm grateful for the service, but I think for that kind of money, he should have least feigned a life-and-death struggle with the rodent.

One last note on this incident. My insurance company confirmed the fact that it will not cover damage done by squirrels, rats, or any domestic animal. However, it's nice to know that if a deer or, God forbid, a cougar gets into my home, they'll pay for all damage to my house and my person. Isn't that a relief ? I know I'll sleep a lot better.

Natural Talents

I am often amazed by the natural gifts people possess. For example, I love to watch the artists who hang out at the mall. They not only draw portraits of live people but they draw perfect portraits from photographs as well. They draw everything from dogs to brides, and they do it in a matter of minutes in front of thousands of curious shoppers. I can't imagine performing well under that kind of scrutiny.

Singing is another talent I envy. I know I don't possess this gift either because those who are near and dear to me have told me so. And I'm sure my family wishes I could sing because I do it often. When my daughter was in grade school, and I would belt out a tune, she reacted in one of two ways: either she covered her ears with her hands or she cranked up the volume of the radio until it drowned out my melodious tones. I used to tell her flat out:

"You can blast that stereo until it shatters every piece of glass in the house. I don't care, and I'm going to keep on singing especially when you have friends over -- just to embarrass you."

This threat was enough to make her run from the room in terror. And people wonder why I never won the Mother of the Year Award yet.

While some talents are not as prestigious as others, they still deserve our respect. For instance, I thinks my daughter, Coleen, has many talents, but one of her strongest is her scream. She has the perfect horror movie scream. She can hold a high-pitched scream for minutes, and she doesn't need to come up for air. I don't want to brag, but I think this is a marketable skill we can exploit in the future. Think of the work she could get in Hollywood. She can not only appear in movies, but she can do voiceovers for all those high-paid performers who don't how to scream.

Coleen's childhood friend, Alicia, could lift up her leg and wrap it around her neck while she was standing up. The kid was double-jointed everywhere, and when she would demonstrate this ability, we would all cringe and say,

"Ick! ick! ick! Doesn't that hurt? I can't watch anymore."

But we did. It was like watching a bad car wreck. You did not want to see it anymore, but you just had to look.

I've noticed my husband Edward also possesses rare talents. He can add numbers in his head faster than anyone I know. I'm talking columns. Of course, he can't spell the word "I", but what does that matter when you're a mathematical whiz kid. He also has a less dignified gift. He can turn his eyelids inside out. While I don't appreciate this talent especially at the dinner table, my daughter and her friends adored it.

"Mr. Cavanagh, do that thing with your eyes!" they would scream. "And being the mature man that he was, he would stop whatever he was doing and invert his eyelids.

Now, talents aren't totally lost on me. I do have one. I can find a stud beam in a wall just by looking at the wall and rubbing my palm over it. I never miss. My husband doesn't hang a picture or a shelf without me locating every possible beam in that wall. I'm not sure where this talent comes from, but my best guess is my grandfather who was a carpenter and bricklayer.

I am the first to admit that finding studs is not a gift that would cause any observer to say,

"Wow, look what she can contribute to that marriage."

But I tell you this: after so many years of marriage, I'm darn proud that I still have a talent that makes my husband say,

"Okay, Hon. Let's do this one together."

The Evil of Optimism

After years of defending the rights and beliefs of optimists everywhere, I have made a remarkable discovery: we optimists are a dying breed. Worse than that, we are an unwanted breed. And as one woman so eloquently put it when I mistakenly tried to cheer her up,

"You are more annoying than fingernails on a chalkboard."

I don't mean to be oversensitive, but I was insulted by that remark. If this woman didn't want to be cheered up, then why the heck did she call me? Obviously, she wanted to share her depression with me. And while I'm appreciative of her generosity, I would prefer that in the future, she hoard that depression for herself. For the record, I didn't mean to minimize her suffering. All I meant to say to her was, "Things are going to get better. You have to trust that life will turn in your favor again."

I'm sorry to say that as much as I have tried and as much as others have tried to convert me, I can't and won't give up on optimism. I can't think that the world is a terrible place, and I won't think that people are selfish beings out only to protect their own hides. Go ahead; feel free to laugh at me. I'll even help you along. I'll share with you some of the more sarcastic questions die hard pessimists have asked me over the years:

- Were you raised in the land of Oz? (No, the Bronx and then New Jersey -- same difference.)

- Was it always a lifelong ambition of yours to be a mouseketeer? (Well, I did always like those ears.)

- Do you think there is a possibility that Shirley Temple could be your sister? (I doubt it. I swear much more than she does. I think.)

And my personal favorite,

- You were a cheerleader -- weren't you? (No, tried out but didn't make the squad. I wasn't peppy enough.)

Oh, I know. I can be just as sarcastic as those who embrace the negative, but it angers me to no end that we can't be happy unless we are wallowing in misery or fearing our demise. For example, one of the top stories this year was the predictions of what would happen in the year 2012.

When that story started to make its way through the internet and news media, some people began to panic and declare that the world would soon end. I'm of the school that says, "We have no control over this kind of stuff so why worry?" Quite frankly, most people have more pressing issues in their lives now to worry about then when the world will finally end.

This is definitely an era that embraces and looks to doomsdayers for advice. Worriers are all over the internet asking "experts" how they should prepare for the end.

Some of you might think that it is easy for me to spout off platitudes about the glory of one's existence. But rest assured, I have not led a Pollyanna life. I've had my struggles -- surprisingly difficult struggles. But I'll be damned if I let those struggles devour my life and turn me into the whiner from hell. And for anyone who mocks my optimism, I say this: you can call me naive or silly. You can say I possess the mentality of a Barbie doll on laughing gas. And to these charges, I have only one

response: Thank   you.   For I know when it comes to
handling life and its unexpected curve balls,   it's the
person who sees the glass as half full-- not half empty --
who triumphs with few if any regrets.

Walking the Tights Rope

Well, I've done it. I've accomplished the one life goal that I swore would elude me my entire life. I am now officially "the meanest mother in the world." How did I win this most auspicious title? I'm not exactly sure what put me over the top, but I think it was a steady combination of nagging and attitude.

See, it all started last fall. For some strange reason, my daughter adopted this crazy habit of removing her uniform tights and throwing them on the living room rug as soon as she walked through my front door after school. Apparently, they bothered her. I understood that. So, the first few times, I would pick up the discarded tights and place them in the hamper. About a week into this stripping routine, I started to get annoyed, and I stated my objections and my request that she remove her own tights from the room.

"Sure, Mom," was her cooperative response. "I'll take care of it as soon as I get something to eat."

I thought that was fair. School always made me hungry. What was another few minutes? However, an hour later, I returned to the living room and lo and behold the tights still lay in the middle of the room. Again, I asked her to remove them. This time, her response was not as cordial.

"All right, I said I'd move them. Why are you in such a bad mood?" she asked in that sort of Clueless - Valley Girl tone. I was taken aback. Frankly, I didn't realize I was in a bad mood. I thought I was just asking for a little bit of cooperation. But to a 10-year-old, with festering hormones, any form of parental correction is synonymous with a bad mood.

As the weeks flew by, my daughter continued to defy me in my request that she strip   closer to the hamper or laundry room. Each day, we would banter back and forth until she would stomp up the stairs with tights in hand. One week, I decided to let the tights stay. I didn't remove them; which meant I didn't wash them.   Not surprisingly, I soon heard the cry as she dressed for school,

"I have no tights. Where are my tights?"

"You want to see tights, I'll show you tights! I'll show you lots of tights!" I took her to the living room and pointed out each pair that she wore within the last few days.

"Like you didn't wash them?"

With all the sarcasm I could muster I said, "Do you see the word 'slave' etched across my chest? Of course I didn't wash them. If you want them clean, you wash them."

"You know..." She stopped short on that sentence when she saw that my patience with her was at an absolute end. I had won the battle. I wallowed in the pleasure of that parental victory. That morning she had to wear one of the dirty pairs on the rug. This totally disgusted her.   For about a month after that, I never saw tights or any other leg wear in my living room.

My celebrations proved short lived. As basketball season rolled in, I started to find pairs of sweat socks hidden behind chairs in the living room. Once again, my nagging commenced. Once again, she ignored my pleas.

Then it hit me. She may be my physical clone, but she is her father's daughter. I decided to attack her where it would hurt most: her pocketbook. Each time she dropped a piece of clothing in any room besides her bedroom, I would confiscate one dollar from her piggy bank. It took ten dollars for her to admit defeat. One dollar she lost out of true forgetfulness; the other nine she lost out of obstinate spite.

This is where I became the meanest mother in the world. I could have said, "I think you've learned your lesson. Take the money back. " But I didn't. I kept the money, and I made her earn it back with more chores than the kid ever thought existed. She did laundry; she changed sheets; she raked the yard; she worked. Even my husband, who tells me I'm too soft on her, felt a pang of sympathy for his beloved princess.

"I feel like Cinderella, and you're the evil stepmother," she cried.

"I know, and it feels so good," I admitted happily.

"You're like the meanest mother in the entire world."

I nodded with pride. For it was then I realized that the rewards of parenthood come from more than love and hard work. It's the sweet acts of revenge that truly make it all worth while.

The Dinner Menu

We have always had a handful of pizza restaurants we liked to patronize. Depending on where we were determined where we would eat. When my daughter was younger, we used to go to this one pizza place after her dance class. We loved this restaurant because it had great place mats. Yep, each week the mats offered a new quiz. These quizzes were fun and made the time between ordering and getting our food pass quickly.

At first, the quizzes were fun. They were geared toward kids and covered topics such as rating a child's behavior at home. The quiz contained questions like: Do you make your bed every day? Do you hang up your clothes? Do you set the table? Do you talk back to your parents? After the quiz, we would total up the score and deliver the scientific news to my daughter. When my daughter scored low on the quizzes, we would laugh them off and tell her not to take them so seriously. After all, any quiz that you take on a place mat, cannot be all that accurate -- right?

The next week, there was yet another new quiz: How Do you rate as a Wife?

This stupid mat had the audacity to want me rate my performance with questions like: Do you get dressed up and look pretty in the morning for your husband?

Is this mat for real? My husband's lucky if I acknowledge his right to live and breathe on the planet in the morning. The man wakes up at 5:30 a.m. Pretty much the only response I have for him at this ungodly hour is,

"Hit the snooze button before I throw the clock out the window!" I bet you're surprised at this, but do you know, that response wasn't even on the test grid, so I had to give myself a zero.

The next question I considered more absurd: Do you make your husband breakfast? Well, he takes extra money to get coffee and doughnuts on his way to work every morning. If that's breakfast, give me the points. Once again "breakfast out" was not assigned any score -- another zero.

The third question: Do you get angry if your husband goes out with the boys after a long day of hard work?

I did good with this one. He is in the golf league, and I never complain about a night out with friends. I recognize he works hard, and he recognizes that I work hard. So, if I make no fuss about him going out then he makes no fuss about me going out, and frankly, I need my nights out, so we compromise. Because of this mature response I got a whopping two points. I was on the board. I was singing and tapping my fork with delight.

Unfortunately, those were the only two points I scored. I lost points to my response to the question: Do you bring your husband snacks when he's relaxing and watching the football game?

"Who is this imbecile who composed this ludicrous test? What is he-- some throwback to the Donna Reed era? Bring him in here! Better yet, bring his wife. We need to have a talk!"

Those two points -- those two, lousy points -- put me in the category of "You need to improve your wifely skills and be more considerate of your man." I can tell you all now, that it took every ounce of control I had in my body not to take the place mat up to the owner of this establishment and shove it in his face and verbally abuse him for his choice of table settings. But I do have a modicum of class and self-restraint.

I took my husband's advice and laughed it off. Then I saw it. Quiz #2: The husband's test. I thought, "Ah, revenge." But his questions were nothing but sheer puff. I was stunned.

Do you tell your wife she's attractive? Do you compliment your wife on her cooking? Do you help your wife discipline the children? Do you bring your wife home flowers for no special occasions?

Pardon me, but where are the beef and grit questions like: Do you pick up your socks and underwear off the floor in the morning? Do you know how to operate the washing machine? Do you know how to locate any object in the house without asking your wife to draw you a detailed map?

Where were these questions? Forget the compliments. I want action. I don't need flowers (but for future reference, I do admire those diamond commercials that show up during the holidays), but I would not mind someone to say, "Hey, Hon, how about if I clean the bathrooms tonight?" I can assure you that this one question would get my husband a lot more than points on a stupid test. For a woman, hearing a man ask if he can actually clean the bathrooms is an important romantic high point in her life. Sad but true. It's on the same scale with hearing a man say, "My God, have you lost weight? You look so thin!"

Let me close on this note. We went back to the restaurant the following Thursday. My husband was nervous, but I promised that I would control myself no matter what was printed on the menus. You know, it's funny. They had a totally different place mat. They had "Find the 50 States" word puzzle for the kids. My guess is that I was not the only woman who commented on the test. I think Mr. Pizza owner may have gotten a tad frightened by his women clientele. Good Job, Ladies. We're all proud!

How to Be a Merry Motorist

Before the days of E-Z Pass, we spent a great deal of time in toll lanes on our journeys to visit family who all lived out of state. During one of our trips, my husband pulled up to the toll booth on the Northeast Extension of the Pennsylvania Turnpike and handed over his usual fare. The toll booth operator uttered a polite thank you and then handed him a turnpike newsletter, brochure and a nifty sheet of driving tips which if followed carefully should make the turnpike a more pleasant road to drive.

Personally, I liked this packet of information. I wasn't exactly sure if it was a good idea to hand out reading material to drivers who are going 65 miles per hour, but I guess that was a chance the turnpike people have to take if they want to get their point across. And their point was this: a happy motorist is a safe motorist. The turnpike people wanted harmony and patience on the road. I think that's a nice thought so to help them out, I would like to share some of their tips that still resound today.

Have your money and ticket ready before you get to the toll window or get E-Z Pass.

Frankly, I don't think this is too much to ask. Who has not been stuck behind a driver who at the toll booth has to search for change? We've all seen these drivers. They stretch out their legs and half stand in their seats while they frantically dig through their pockets for money. Sometimes, they're struggling so much to get their hands in their pockets that they fail to notice that their stretched out foot has pressed down on the gas pedal. Before they realize what's happening, their flying through the toll lane at warp speed. Then all the drivers behind them have to wait for them to back up to the window again and pay their fare. What's worse than these drivers are the women who empty their purses on the passenger seat -- or their passenger -- all in an effort to find that necessary change. One time, I had a woman in front of me ask the toll operator to hold her compact and lipstick so she could find her money at the bottom of her purse.

Please refrain from talking on your cell phone while paying the toll.

I can't believe that this has to be a written request. But apparently, many a driver doesn't think toll booth operators deserve our full attention. And this is a shame. It's not easy being stuck in a booth for eight hours a day. The only conversation some of these operators have are the ones with the drivers. So hang up that phone before you pay your toll and give that toll booth worker an enthusiastic smile and greeting.

Plan your approach to the booths. If the road is clear, get into the lane with the fewest vehicles. Use turn signals to do this.

Honestly, I see problems with this request. Few of us waiting in the toll booth lines trust our fellow drivers. If the lines are long, our eyes dart between other motorists and the toll booths to see if a new lane is getting ready to open up. As soon as the little green light on top of the booth goes on, we're ready to make our move. We want to be the first person in the new lane. But as any experienced toll lane driver will tell you, you can't be the first person in the new lane if you give the other drivers notice by using your turn signals. Using a turn signal robs a driver of the element of surprise. Using a turn signal in the toll lane goes against the unspoken code of the toll lane driver which says: "Anything is fair when you're trying to be first in line!" You would think the turnpike people would know this. The toll booth lane is a jungle. And those who can't drive in that jungle shouldn't take toll roads; they should take the back roads.

Drivers should all be patient with people who ask directions at the toll booth.
In my opinion, I think people who ask directions at toll booths during the week day rush hour should be banned from driving forever. I understand that people get lost, but this is why God made GPS systems. If you do not have a GPS system, get off at an exit and find a gas station. . If toll booth operators were meant to give directions, they'd have maps or at least an AAA office in their booths with them.

It would be nice if we could all just get along on the road. Perhaps the turnpike people are right. Maybe if we smile at our fellow motorists and our dedicated turnpike personnel and maybe if every once in a while we let a fellow motorist cut in front of us, we would be better drivers.

Personalizing our Lives

A few weeks ago, I sat at a red light behind a zippy, little, German-made convertible. Immediately, I was attracted to this adorable luxury vehicle, and my mind wandered as I tried to imagine what its owner looked like. Within seconds a picture of Mel Gibson popped into my head, and this image made me like this car even more. I was in seventh heaven until I saw IT. There it was in big letters staring me in the face -- a personalized license plate which read only "Zrpunk." (Please note, some letters may have been changed to conceal the true identity of the driver.)

Needless to say, the picture of Mel Gibson quickly transformed itself into a picture of Bozo the Clown. I was devastated. How could this guy do this to me? Perfect, fantasy men don't have vanity plates -- especially vanity plates that hold some secret code which only he and his small circle of friends understand. Obviously, this guy's name wasn't "Zrpunk", so what did it mean?

I know, it's a silly pet peeve, but why do people spend the extra fee to have a special license plate made which displays a message no one comprehends. I think it's somewhat rude. It's like being left out of a secret club. If the politeness issue doesn't phase you, what about the traffic safety factor? We've all been on the road when the car in front of us --with a vanity plate -- catches our eye. Do we ignore it? No. We are drawn to it, and we try to decipher the meaning behind the mystery message. To do this, we close in on the car until we see the vanity plate clearly. By now, we're tailgating. Then we sit there like fools mouthing aloud the sounds of the vowels, consonants and numbers until the meaning of the message reaches our brains. (You can always tell the people who just deciphered a vanity plate. They have that "light bulb just clicked on" look all over their face, and they are beaming with pride.) What's sad is that for some of us, this is the high point of our day. Before we know it, we're slamming on our brakes trying to avoid a rear-end collision with the vanity plate and its driver.

I understand that vanity plates can serve a vital purpose. Many people use them to tell the driving world what they do for a living. For instance, how could we tell that the driver of the Mercedes cruising passed us at 90 M.P.H. is a physician unless his or her plate is marked with that oversized M.D.? If the plate didn't have those markings, we would think that driver was just another speed-crazy jerk. Instead, we sit there and say, "Hey, it's okay. That guy is a doctor."

Truth be told, vanity plates that display one's profession don't impress anyone. If your goal is to show people you've made it, or you're important, don't display your job; display your income tax return. Just put your gross salary on the plate. I'm sure if you do that, you can attract an amazing number of people from all walks of life.

Of all those people who have these special plates, the ones I worry about the most are those who have their full names displayed. Are these people afraid they won't be able to find their cars in a parking lot unless they're labeled? I bet these are the same people who have name tags in their underwear and monograms on all their shirts and towels. Do they have a fear they're going to lose these things or have them stolen right off their backs? Maybe they're afraid they're going to forget who they are.

If they are afraid of theft, a personalized license plate is not going to deter a thief or make it easier to find a thief. Even a bad thief would know to dump the license plate before taking the car on a long joy ride. And that goes double for the monogrammed shirts, underwear and towels. How many thieves would even want used, intimate apparel? So, what are these personalized items there for?

Once again, we're back to status. It's been said that everyone wants to achieve some sort of fame in life. Maybe that's what vanity plates are all about. When John Doe drives down the street in his car with his vanity plate, people know who he is. He experiences a feeling of importance. People recognize him. Most don't care who he is, but they still recognize him. He has achieved fame in a pitiful sort of way.

You can call me cynical or over-protective, but I still think it's best not to draw too much attention to yourself on the road. I think everyone should abide by some sort of privacy code when driving. You can wave and honk at people you know, you can sing out loud and pound out the beat of your favorite tune on your steering wheel, and you can even giggle at the funny DJs who grace the airwaves each day. But you shouldn't be allowed to introduce yourself via your license plate to all the other people on the road. The whole motoring process requires an enormous amount of concentration, and the majority of us are not that adept at it. We don't need any more distractions than are already out there. So, I think for the sake of everyone, we should all go back to the plain, simple license plates which make us all equal and which cause no fuss, no curiosity and no collisions.

Volunteering Is a Risky Business

I have often heard it said that to be a true volunteer, one must possess a good heart and a good soul. To this list of requirements I'd like to add four more vital ones: a strong stomach, a thick skin, bad hearing and an overwhelming desire to be yelled at. For these are the traits by which the true volunteer survives and hopefully returns to give again.

Oh, I know how cynical this sounds, but human beings are a predictable lot. We love to complain and moan. We're not happy unless we're angry about something. And we're less happy if we can't voice that anger to some poor sap who thought it would be nice to give his or her time to a cause.

Case in point: our daughter's softball league. For years, it was the same people who volunteered to be coach, commissioner, team parents or field maintenance crew. And it was the same people who found fault with every policy and decision made by this team of volunteers. I have to say, I grew pretty sick of complaints. Each year, the league leaders begged people to come on board, and each year the same faces answered that plea. So, one year, I put into practice a new way of dealing with the moaners and groaners who came to voice their criticism. Let me tell you how my first experience with this went.

A parent called me at my home and complained that she did not approve of the days of the week our league played games because it interfered with other activities of her daughter. Before I go any further, let me say that I made every attempt to display as much courtesy to this woman as possible.

"My daughter has piano on Wednesdays. She can't be there. Can't you change the days of the games to Tuesdays?"

"Well, we'd like to oblige, Ma'am. But we only have the fields on Wednesdays and Fridays. We're pretty much committed to those days."

"Well, that is so inconvenient," she responded in a rather indignant tone. "What should my daughter do?"

"Can you change the day of her piano lessons for the season?"

I didn't think that was an outlandish request. But the dead silence on the other end of the phone forced me to assume she didn't like this idea. I assumed right. From the reaction of this mother, you would have thought I asked her to fly to the moon without a rocket. She laid into me about the importance of her daughter's musical education. She explained loudly that it cost a lot of money to give her child this musical experience. I tried to explain back that 75 other girls could make it on Wednesdays and Fridays, and it would be in the best interest of the league to go with their schedule. Even after explaining this point to this woman, she still didn't get it. To her, I was an evil woman whose sole purpose in life was to impede the musical and athletic talents of her daughter. Stupid me, I should have understood. You see, her daughter is the most special daughter put on the face of the earth. All the other girls of the world were just placed here to give her kid some company. Once I understood that concept, I knew exactly where this woman was coming from.

This is where I became less gracious. I know, I shouldn't have said it, but I come from an Italian family, and we're just not good at holding things in.

"Ma'am," I made sure to start out my ranting in a low-toned voice. I raised my volume ever so slightly as I got further into my speech. "Did you volunteer to do anything for our league? I don't think I saw your name down as commissioner. Are you a coach or an assistant coach or a team parent or a snack stand parent?" No response. I had her on the ropes, and I gave her no slack. "No? Oh, I see. You must be the person who is heading up the bitching committee."

I think I may have insulted her. Gee, my heart breaks. After that, she said very little to me. In fact, I haven't heard from her again.

For the record, I have been and may be again an offender of the very same thing I am complaining about. But I have learned that if I have the energy to complain, then I have the energy to help out. I think that's a philosophy we should all try to adopt.

When Everything Falls Apart

I can't even tell you how it happened. One minute I'm cruising behind the wheel of my husband's car, singing along to a Bruce Springsteen tune on the radio and the next minute, I'm watching in disbelief as the windshield disintegrated before my eyes. Okay, it didn't exactly disintegrate. The bottom of the windshield sort of splintered in all different directions. Using my keen sense of observation, I ascertained that some foreign object, possibly a piece of meteor, blew out of the sky and plummeted to the earth landing on the car -- or -- the windshield may have fell victim to a stone from the uncovered gravel truck traveling just inches ahead of me on the road. Personally, I was rooting for the meteorite. I thought a more dramatic story, which didn't include me tailgating, would win sympathy points with the man who entrusted me with his precious vehicle. I thought for sure he couldn't blame a person who was almost obliterated by fiery lava from space.

Apparently, I was wrong. You can be blamed for errant meteors if they land on your windshield. Both my husband and my insurance company told me so. Who knew? Anyway, I survived the tailgating lecture and the "Can you be more careful with my car?" speech. Eventually, we both did our best to forget about the damage which was no easy feat considering the spidery crack on the bottom of the windshield served as a constant reminder of my rendezvous with the gravel truck.

Just days later, my husband took my car and went off to work. That morning, I get the call.

"The weirdest thing happened," he starts off with a chuckle in his voice. "You know how there is so much construction on the turnpike? Well, in one of the heavier construction zones, a rock flew up and smashed into your windshield. It's pretty much cracked all over. We'll have to get it replaced as soon as possible."

Pause. He was waiting for my reaction. I had two choices. I could be the vengeful spouse and harangue him on the correct way to maneuver a vehicle around trucks and rocks. Or, I could be a supportive spouse and remind him that these incidents occur all the time and no one is to blame. Believe it or not, in a moment I can only describe as pure inspiration, I chose to be supportive.

Why? Because I knew it would bug the hell out of him. He expected me to yell and carry on. What fun would it have been to act as he was prepared for me to act? Being supportive threw him off guard. If I yelled, I would be the mean one, and he would feel no guilt. There was no way I was going to let that happen. For days, I had the upper hand in our marriage. I was in control, and he felt shame and remorse. He was so nice and considerate; it was as if we were dating again. It was a dream come true. During that blissful time, the man never argued with me or made suggestions about anything including my sometimes sloppy banking habits. Never in my life had I inflicted so much guilt on one person. It felt wonderful!

But alas, all good things must come to an end. The windshields got fixed, and we had settled back into our usual marriage pattern where neither of us had anything to hold over the other. Life had returned to normal until fate dealt me a wicked blow. Within the same week, my coffee maker and my dishwasher went on the fritz; my washing machine decided it didn't want to spin anymore, and the computer in his car crashed

Initially, the onslaught of all these breakdowns left us in a state of shock. Then, as we began to estimate the damage, we looked for ways to lay the blame for these mishaps at the feet of the other. In our minds, we were sure someone had to be responsible for all this turmoil. It's easier to accept misfortune if someone is to blame. But as we came to grips with the repair bills from these unfortunate occurrences, we toughened up, shrugged our shoulders and gave each other some slack. What else could we do? Machines may always fall apart. But we both know that we never will.

When Do Mothers Become Leaders Of The Pack?

Recently, I watched a show on public television about wolves. When I say I watched this show, I mean I watched it. The program mesmerized me. It wasn't that I found the wolves' lives to be so exciting. Oh, sure they hunt and howl and live in the woods, but that's not what grabbed my interest. What caught my attention was the pack's family structure. I realized about ten minutes into this show that these wolves were living my life. I could have pasted pictures of my family's heads on to those wolves' bodies, and I would swear I was watching home movies. How could that be? Well, let me explain. And after I explain, I'm willing to wager that there are many wives and mothers out there who feel the same way I do.

According to this program, in each pack of wolves there is an alpha wolf, the middle or beta wolves, and the omega wolf. The alpha wolf is the male -- of course (How does this always happen?) The pack revolves around his needs and wants. Does this sound familiar to anyone out there so far? He struts around telling the females of the pack that he is in charge. They, in turn concede to his every wish. He enlists one female to be his companion and the producer and caretaker of his offspring. In all fairness, the alpha wolf does have certain responsibilities. He must go out and hunt for food. Sometimes, some of the other wolves help him with this task, but he is considered head honcho. And as head honcho, he gets first pick of all the food that comes into the pack. Only when the alpha wolf has dined to his heart's content, do the beta wolves get to eat. And once they are done, the last scraps are devoured by the pack sap -- the omega wolf.

I am not saying my family life is this primitive. I'm not saying my husband is that egotistical alpha wolf. But I have to admit, as I watched that show, I keenly identified with that poor omega wolf. Everyone else's needs came before the omega, and no one thought twice about letting that happen.

Don't misread my observations. I'm not complaining I don't get enough food or that my husband takes all the good cuts of meat and leaves me with nothing but grizzle and lean leftovers. Frankly, I get more than my share of leftovers. In fact, I get everyone's leftovers. I wish someone would cut off my supply so my sojourns to the scale wouldn't be quite so painful. But that's another story. No, my comparisons to the wolf pack are figurative.

What I am saying is that sometimes I want someone to say to me -- preferably someone in my family

"Damn, look how you sacrifice so that we, your pack may thrive."

Yes, I want to hear those words, and not only on Mother's Day. I'm not trying to man bash, nor are my comments a silent cry for pity. Actually, they are a loud cry for pity, and I hope someone out there is listening. I want -- as do many wives and mothers -- the chance to be the first at the dining table. I want to know what it's like to buy something for me without feeling like I wasted money that should have gone to my daughter's orthodontist or the dry cleaning bill. I want to go shopping and do more than just try on. I want to buy -- for me.

I know, I am pathetic because in all honesty, it is me who has made myself the omega wolf, and I venture to say that most women who feel as I do, have put themselves into the same position. Somewhere along the line, we learned that being a good mother or wife meant that our needs have to come last. I think we women not only tolerate this idea, but we pass it on to our daughters.

Is there a remedy for this? I guess we could chant some feminist rhetoric which hopefully would inspire both sexes to change their way of thought. Or, we could get up the courage and knock the alpha and beta wolves right off their thrones and on to their furry, little tails. Let them handle the omega's responsibilities for a while. Let them fetch and clean the food. Let them care for the young pups. Let them handle everything themselves. After a few days, those alpha and betas will beg all us omegas to come home. They'll promise us the world, and you know what we'll say?

"Okay, what do you want me to get for dinner?"

Alas --once a wolf pack sap, always a wolf pack sap.

All Employees Need Training

I think it is a safe bet that if you work for a corporation, you will go to some kind of training class at least once a year. In my small office, it is no different. I expect my employees, be they man or beast, to be computer literate. My employees – my dogs -- must keep their computer skills sharp as well.

Ah, you scoff? Why shouldn't my dogs learn PowerPoint or at least Word. They already answer the fax and are adept at retrieving paper from the printer. Why then, shouldn't they be able to listen to a presentation or even give one themselves especially when I am so busy and can use a few extra paws around the office?

Yes, my pooches want to hold on to their positions. After all, they stink at typical doggie duties, so they might as well master human ones. I think as they learn more about technology, I'll give them added responsibility. Maybe I can give them a press release or two to write to see how they do. They can write on subjects they know: dog treats, which bird feeders attract the most winged prey to the yard or even the best tasting mulch for the garden. How they love mulch!

Okay, maybe I am asking too much of them. After all, I guess they really can't do a PowerPoint presentation. Can they? Can dogs be trained for things like this? When I see a dog on television, I am amazed at what a trainer can accomplish. Dogs can be stars of movies and TV shows. They can cops and firefighters. They can work with the military in demolition units. They rescue people who are buried in six feet of snow during avalanches. Why can't they be more business minded?

Do you know what I could save on outsourcing fees if my dogs could pick up the slack for me? I don't think they would hit me with an outrageous hourly wage. My guess is a good steak once a week would do the trick for them. And I wouldn't be a strict boss. Already, if they are not barking at the fax or printer, I let them take hour-long power naps. They even get to take two-hour lunch breaks in the yard. I think they got it made in the shade!

Clients might appreciate a canine computer whiz. A canine geek would probably be more accessible than most customer service reps. They wouldn't be rude or judgmental. They would listen for long periods of time. They wouldn't put people on hold for an hour and force them to endure the Muzak version of "Muskrat Love." Of course, they might accidentally commit sexual harassment by deep breathing and panting into the phone. I guess to avoid law suits, I would confine them to email only.

I think this idea could work. I think a lot of people would be delighted to get email from my dogs as long as they exhibited a professional manner. I think it would take the edge off this highly technological world we live in. It would add a little "humanity." This may be an idea that has a few bugs to work out yet, but I'm not giving up on the idea. In the meantime, I will continue to keep my dogs as current as possible on advances in technology. Mark my words, one day, they will be knows as DEOs or Doggie Executive Officers. Who will have the last laugh then?

Yard Sale: the Price is Not Right

Recently, I got into one of my frenzied cleaning moods. Usually, when this happens, I find relief in a bottle of Windex and some Brillo pads. But this time, I needed to do more than clean -- I needed to clean out. So, I announced to my husband and daughter that we were going to have a yard sale.

At the mere mention of this event, the two of them dashed off to parts of the house they had not yet discovered: the basement, the attic and the bottom of their closets. Their mission: to gather, hide and protect their valuables from my wrath.

"You want to sell our belongings?" they asked in disbelief.

"No," I answered curtly. "I want to sell our junk."

"But I don't want to sell my stuff. I still use it," my husband moaned.

"Yeah, I see how handy this 1976 New York Yankee yearbook has been through the years, " I said sarcastically. " It works so well as a cobweb catcher in the back of the basement."

"I still look at it," he insisted.

I knew this was not an arguable point. He was living in denial and the only way to snap him out of it was to prove to him that his yearbook was worthless. I gave him the number of a baseball memorabilia collector and told him to call. Within two minutes he came back wearing a "dreams smashed to smithereens" look on his face.

"What happened?" I asked with sincere compassion.

"It's not worth anything." he muttered.

Being the sap I am, I caved.

"Okay, you can keep the yearbook if you try really hard to clear out your shop and the attic. Is that a deal?"

He happily agreed and bopped away in victory.

Next, I turned my attention to my daughter, Coleen, who had barricaded herself in the Barbie room.

"I'm not selling any of my Barbies! You can't have them."

"I don't want any of your 62,000 dolls," I reassured her. "I want the stuff you don't play with anymore. The baby stuff. "

"But what if I want to play with them again someday? Then I won't have them."

All I could think at this point was "Here we go again. Like father like daughter. This kid may look like me, but her brain works just like her father's."

To handle my charming and obstinate child, I took a different approach.

"C.C., let's talk money. Any money made from the sale of your toys goes directly to you. You can do whatever you want with it. It doesn't have to go in the bank."

After I put that promise in writing, she dashed off to clear out her room, the Barbie room, the family room and any other room that held her belongings. I finally had them in the yard sale spirit.

I'll admit right now I got a bit carried away with this sale. I now understand why my family expressed such concern when I mentioned my desire to host one of these events. Edward says I possessed a greedy glint in my eye whenever I passed an object in the house that had the potential of wearing a price tag.

For weeks before the sale, my family heard the same questions over and over.

"Do we need that dresser? Do we need that coffee table? Do we need that bed? Do we need that car?"

Okay, so I got scary.

My husband, who is probably the most patient man on Earth, argued repeatedly with me.

"If you sell that, we have to replace it which means ---what?" he would ask leadingly.

"It means we buy new stuff," I answered matter of factly.

"But it will cost us more to replace the old stuff!"

As if logic was going to bring me down.

"So?"

"So? We'll be in hock for years."

Leave it to him to find the negatives in all this. Anyway, we had the yard sale, and I tried my best to sell stuff I no longer wanted in the house. I put tags on the coffee table, my husband's worn out recliner and even his T-bird. People came, looked and bought. But alas, no one bought these items. At the end of the day, we dragged them back into the house, and we pulled the car back on to the driveway. My husband sat in his recliner and emitted the loudest sigh of relief I have ever heard. He was a happy man. He had his chair, his coffee table and his car. They were still safe.

"You know," he said to me triumphantly. "This was a great sale. We should do it again next year."

Morning at the Cable Company

This morning, I readied myself. I put on my brightest Christmas sweater, I practiced my cheeriest disposition in the mirror and I stretched the muscles in my face so that I could deliver my warmest smile on a moment's notice. Yes, I had participated in painstaking preparations, and now I was prepared to face the toughest challenge that exists in the world today: The women behind the front desk at the cable TV office.

This was the situation. I had signed up for one of the cable company's promotions where I got internet, TV and phone service for a low introductory price. As an extra nice gesture, the cable salesperson also tossed in two DVRs. The one in my bedroom never really worked. I did not care while it was free, but when the six-month promotion was over, I decided to trade in the broken DVR for a regular HD box and save myself a few pennies on my bill. Normally, when I go to the cable TV company, I take my husband with me for moral support. I admit that I am scared of these women. I would rather get a colonoscopy than deal with these women. I don't know why the cable company puts them in the front to deal with people. I truly believe they want to scare people away.

But alas, today I was on my own, so I decided to fight fire with honey. I decided that I was going to be the sweetest person that they ever did see. No arguments were going to emanate from my mouth. I was going to be their most cooperative customer of the year – or at least the day.

I stepped into the cable office with broken DVR in hand and I was amazed that there was no line in front of the bullet proof windows. Yes, the bullet proof windows. I am in the middle of suburbia. I go to banks, the post office, credit unions and fast food restaurants where there is always a lot of cash on hand, and do they have bullet proof windows? NO. But the cable office does. What does that say when the cable company needs bullet proof partitions?

Anyway, I was so amazed and focused on the fact that there was no line that I missed the sign at the entrance which said, "PRESS A BUTTON TO TELL US WHY YOU ARE HERE."

With a spring in my step, I went up to one of the windows and started to talk to the woman wearing the microphone headset behind the partition. BIG MISTAKE. Immediately she waved me away and shouted at me through her microphone to step behind the console and press the button. She looked mad too. Rats, this mistake would cost me. I had already ruffled her feathers! I began to get that sick feeling in my stomach. But I persevered. I retreated to the console and pressed the TV button to tell her I needed help with my cable. I heard a buzz and then the woman ordered me, again through the microphone, to step up to the glass. She also instructed me to open the glass door on the side of her partition, slide in my DVR equipment and shut the door behind it. When I had completed her instructions, she then opened another door on her side and removed my cable equipment and shut and locked the door on her side. I guess these are all precautions every cable person needs to take, but I'm thinking Homeland Security could learn a thing or two from these people. I never realized how dangerous being a cable office person could be. Here, I thought it was only the technicians who messed with the electricity and wires who took risks.

Then she asked the fateful question: "Why are you here?"

I did not mince words or make my answer too elaborate. "This DVR box does not work as a DVR and my promotion is up and I wanted to trade it in for an HD box instead," The words flowed so effortlessly that I started to get my confidence back about this whole encounter. Then, she did something I will always remember. She turned the DVR box over and glared at me.

"You don't have a DVR box here. The reason it didn't work is because it is not a DVR box. All you have is an HD box. You wasted your time and mine."

Uh oh. Foiled by my own stupidity. She was getting ready to yell now. I could feel it. She grabbed a DVR box from behind the counter and shoved it close to the partition. Then with her fingers, she showed me the letters DVR and then promptly asked me where on my box did I see those letters.

"Nowhere. My mistake," I said apologetically.

"You bet it is your mistake. You people come in here without knowing what you got at home."

"Again, I am sorry. It was entirely my fault," I said again while smiling.

I have to say that this woman seemed a little more compassionate than the other women I've encountered in this office – all of whom I'm pretty sure moonlight as maximum security prison guards, but what do I know?

Just to drive her final humiliating point home, she decided to look up my bill and informed me that my account file never said I had two DVRs. I was not in fact paying any extra for a second DVR box. She instructed me to go home and check all my other boxes to make sure I didn't put another DVR box in another room and forgot about it.

I wanted to argue back to say I wouldn't forget a thing like that, but she was absolutely in control here, and I did not want to rock the boat. I am always afraid that if you tick off these women too much, they might add stuff to your account that you can never get off. It's just a cable phobia I have.

Then, she told me to step away from the partition while she opened her door and pushed my non-DVR box back to me in the side compartment. When she locked her side, I removed my box and waited for permission to leave. When she said I was done, I thought I would try one more time to bring cheer to the cable office.

With the most positive tone I could muster I said, "Thank you so much for your help and information. I hope you have a wonderful Christmas."

I caught her off guard, and I could see the thaw occur right in front of my eyes. She looked at me with a shocked smile on her face. Yep, I got a smile from a cable lady.

Then, she said, "You too and God bless."

I got a "God Bless". I have to say that I left that cable office feeling pretty satisfied with myself. I had worn down one of the toughest people known to mankind. Sure, she thinks I am a stupid toad because I thought I had a broken DVR box for six months when in reality I never even had a DVR box. But so what? She smiled at me.

As I was leaving the building, a man was coming in and he said. "How are they today?" And I said, "I got a smile." He stopped and actually congratulated me. For a brief moment, I was a hero.

Proof

Made in the USA
Charleston, SC
02 January 2010